LIVING IN ENGLAND

CHAUCER'S ENGLAND

DUNCAN TAYLOR

New York
ROY PUBLISHERS

By the same author:
Living in England: The Elizabethan Age

Second Impression 1962

Copyright © 1959 by Duncan Taylor

Library of Congress Catalog Card No. 60-6642

Printed in Great Britain

92

LIVING IN ENGLAND

CHAUCER'S
ENGLAND

A fourteenth-century banquet with men on horseback riding among the tables.

To

BARBARA

CONTENTS

LIST OF PLATES

List of Plates

ENDPAPERS

Front: Early fourteenth-century embroidery showing the Nativity, the angel appearing to the shepherds (one of whom plays a bagpipe) and the visit of the Magi.
(Victoria and Albert Museum)

Back: Gough Map (see page 37). *c.* 1300
(Bodleian Library, Oxford)

Many of the illustrations in the text have been redrawn from contemporary manuscripts.

INTRODUCTION

IN SEPTEMBER 1327 three wicked men and their escort became the unwelcome guests of Thomas, Lord of Berkeley Castle in Gloucestershire. Two of the men were knights, Sir Thomas Gurney and Sir John Maltravers. The third man was King Edward II, but the knights were not at his side to serve him. On the contrary, he was their prisoner.

No one is ever very keen to kill a king. Superstition and fear of the consequences hold back the most hardened. So Sir Thomas and Sir John put Edward in one of the towers of the castle and stacked rotting corpses of animals in the room below. They thought the stench would do their murder for them. But it did not. They had to do it themselves.

Lord Thomas Berkeley, who had shown himself friendly towards the King, was forced to go and live elsewhere. Then, one night, Sir Thomas and Sir John, with their accomplices, surprised the King in his sleep, smothered his screams with featherbeds and killed him. They announced, however, that he had died a natural death and he was buried in Gloucester Cathedral (Plate VII).

Next year, 1328, Edward III, aged sixteen, married Philippa of Hainault (now part of Belgium). She was about fourteen, tall and handsome. Edward was still King in name only. He had no power. His mother and her favourite, Mortimer, ruled England.

In 1330, aged eighteen, Edward III led a night attack on Nottingham Castle, through an underground passage, and took Mortimer prisoner. Towards the end of November, Mortimer was hanged at Tyburn (near Marble Arch Underground Station in modern London). It was then that Edward's rule over England began. In the same year Queen Philippa bore her first child, Edward, known as the Black Prince. In 1346, when the Black Prince was sixteen, he helped his father to win the battle of Crecy, against the French. The news of this victory must have been one of the earliest memories of a boy who was growing up in the City of London. His name was Geoffrey Chaucer.

Chaucer

Chaucer was born about 1340 and lived through the reigns of Edward III and Richard II. This was the period of the Hundred Years War, which went on intermittently from 1338 to 1453, of the Black Death (1349) and of the Peasants' Revolt (1381). It was a period in which Wycliffe called for reforms in the Church and English replaced French as the language of England. About the year 1387 Chaucer wrote, in English, the *Canterbury Tales*.

Introduction

The English of the *Canterbury Tales* is so different from what we know today that a modern version is called a 'translation'. Nevil Coghill's is good (published by Penguin Books, 1951). For example, the following lines, from Chaucer's description of a miller,

> *Upon the cop right of his nose he hade*
> *A werte and theron stood a toft of herys,*
> *Reed as the brustles of a sowes erys;*

are translated

> *And, at its very tip, his nose displayed*
> *A wart on which there stood a tuft of hair*
> *Red as the bristles in an old sow's ear.*

Those who have not read Chaucer at school may do well to start by using a translation.

Chaucer's father was a wine-merchant in London, sufficiently prosperous to be able to have his son taught to read and write and then to place him as a page in the household of one of the sons of Edward III. That was the best one could do for a teenage boy at the time. Getting him into a noble household was more or less the equivalent of getting him into a good school nowadays.

When he was about twenty Chaucer served in France, was taken prisoner and ransomed. For the rest of his life he earned money by holding a number of official posts, which his good start in life had put him in a position to obtain from the King. For some years he was in charge of customs (payments made on imported

13

goods) at the Port of London. Later he had to supervise the repair of walls, ditches and sewers between Greenwich and Woolwich. He was Clerk of the Works (p. 70) for short periods at Westminster and Windsor.

An inn at night

He made two journeys to Italy on official business. He married and had a son.

Chaucer's duties apparently left him plenty of time for reading and writing. There was not yet much to be read in English but he knew Italian and French. He began by translating a French romance—a long poem telling of heroic men and beautiful women. Poetry was what he enjoyed writing. Among his collected works there is very little prose.

The *Canterbury Tales* are stories, mostly in verse, imagined as being told by a number of pilgrims, who started for Canterbury from the Tabard Inn, Southwark, on the south side of the Thames, in April, 1387. In the *Prologue* to the *Canterbury Tales* the pilgrims—a party of about thirty—are introduced.

The *Prologue* is now the most popular part of Chaucer's work. None of the introductions goes on for too long. Each is a clear picture. But this clearness is not just a matter of being told the colour of the hairs on the wart on the miller's nose. Such details are interesting, but they are not enough. What makes the *Prologue* enjoyable is that Chaucer gives us a fairly clear idea about whether he liked each character or not. He disliked quite a number of the party.

The Age of Chaucer

If one wants to write a book about England in the time of Edward III and Richard II and does not want to call it 'The Age of Edward III and Richard II', because that is rather a clumsy title to squeeze on to a dustcover, there are a number of possibilities. For instance the last two thirds of the fourteenth century might be called the Age of any of the following:

Geoffrey Chaucer, poet	*c.* 1340-1400
John Froissart, historian,	1338- *c.* 1410

John of Gaunt, brother of the
  Black Prince,   1340-1399
John Wycliffe, priest and reformer, *c*. 1324-1384
William of Wykeham, bishop, states-
  man, founder of Winchester College
  and of New College, Oxford,   *c*. 1323-1404
William Langland, poet who wrote
  The Vision of Piers Plowman, *c*. 1332- *c*. 1400
John Trevisa, one of the earliest
  writers of English prose,   1326-1402

All these and other men and women of the time come
into this book; but Chaucer comes into the title because
he is probably better loved than any of them and because in the course of the book his characters are
often referred to.

Chaucer's imaginary characters are often referred to,
because the period covered by this book is one from
which no diaries or collections of personal letters have
come down to us. We have no biographies nor auto-
biographies, no novels and no plays (except for a certain number on religious subjects, p. 138). It is therefore
not easy to build up a picture of the life of Chaucer's
time and it is worth examining the *Prologue* characters,
and those in the tales which follow, very closely, for
evidence.

It would be nice to find a letter from a woman who
really lived in the fourteenth century, describing the
colour of her stockings; but failing this we must turn

I (Above)
  Edward, the Black Prince
(Below)
  Canterbury Cathedral

King Edward III

Geoffrey Chaucer

Tomb of the Black Prince; above which hang his gauntlets, jupon,(a shirt embroidered with his coat of arms), helm, and shield

II Canterbury, West Gate (1380)

The Walls of York

14th Century bridge with chapel, Wakefield (Yorks)

to one of the *Prologue* characters, the Wife of Bath. We find that

Hir hosen weren of fyn scarlet reed

i.e. her hosen (stockings) were of fine scarlet red. They matched her face, which is described as 'bold' and 'reed of hewe' (red in colour).

Even about the life of a person as famous as Chaucer himself, we really know very little. How did he fare during the Black Death? What were his schooldays like? Who were his friends? What did he think about the Peasants' Revolt? What sort of a woman was his wife? How much of the *Canterbury Tales* did he know by heart? Could he recite hundreds of lines or did he have to read aloud? We do not know.

However, there is a great deal that we do know about the period. Thanks to the patient work of many scholars, we can answer a good many questions about living in England in Chaucer's time.

Living in England

This book may be compared to a travel book about some country far away—call it Arimazpia. Different readers expect different things of such a book. Some want to use it only for reference. They want to know, for instance, whether goat's milk is a favourite drink amongst the adult population of Arimazpia. They want to know how many Arimazpians can read and write. What, they ask, are the chief industries of Arimazpia?

This kind of question may equally well be asked about fourteenth-century England and this book tries to provide helpful answers. By all means use it for reference. There is a long index.

There are, however, other readers of travel books who want to enjoy them in bed or in a deck-chair. They want a book to read rather than an encyclopedia to study. I have tried to cater for them too. It is possible to read this book straight through in one or two sittings.

Suppose, however, that the reader is so moved by his travel book that he wants to leap from his deck-chair and take the next boat for Arimazpia? Good luck to him. But he cannot take the next boat for the fourteenth century. What then? For him this book can become a guide to the remains of the fourteenth century which survive in the twentieth. The opening paragraphs have perhaps inspired him to set aside half a crown for a visit to Berkeley Castle during the summer months, when it is open to the public, and to go on to see Edward II's alabaster tomb in Gloucester Cathedral. There is plenty of fourteenth-century building work still to be seen up and down the country. There are also fourteenth-century books—either the real, rich thing, copied by hand, sumptuously illustrated and protected by glass in a museum, or a paper-backed reprint of Chaucer on a second-hand bookstall. You can stare at the first or read the second, or both.

And the Canterbury pilgrimage? The Dover Road

(A2), by which Chaucer's company travelled, is sometimes crowded now. We are promised a double-track motorway to relieve it. In the meantime, however, it is still possible to regain in some measure the position of a fourteenth-century horseman by riding on the top of the bus from Faversham. If the weather is fine, you catch a first glimpse of the cathedral from the hill beyond Harbledown. (From here some pilgrims proceeded barefoot, but Chaucer's jolly party are not likely to have gone to such lengths.) The West Gate, through which you enter Canterbury was new in Chaucer's time. (For 6d adults, for 1d children may climb its massive towers.)

In the cathedral, Becket's gorgeous shrine has gone. Henry VIII made a clean sweep of it. But beside the now empty space where Becket lay, at the top of the steps which the knees of pilgrims hollowed, stands the tomb of the Black Prince. He was only forty-six when he died (1376). Great hopes had been held of what he might do. In England he was well beloved. When the peasants broke into the cathedral in the revolt of 1381, they left his tomb alone. Perhaps, had he lived, we would now attach his name instead of Chaucer's to the later years of the fourteenth century and speak of that time as the first Edwardian age.

But Edward, the Black Prince, died—after a long illness during which there was time for him to give some thought to his place of burial. He chose Canterbury and directed, with military precision, that

19

his body should lie ten feet from the altar of the chapel in the crypt. After he was dead, however, the public would not allow his tomb to lie so low. He must be buried, they felt, beside Becket's shrine. No other place would do.

'The knightly hero of the English people', 'the flower of English chivalry' the Black Prince is called on the notice placed beside his tomb for the information of visitors. The Norman-French inscription on the tomb itself is not easy to read but, we are told, it may be summed up in these few English words:

Thus the glory of this world passes away.

CHAPTER I

LONDON AND ENGLAND

'THE OFFICIAL MEASURING point for London mileages is now Charing Cross.' These words, hidden away amongst much interesting information in the Handbook of the Automobile Association, now surprise no one. Charing Cross, a monument standing in front of the railway station near Trafalgar Square, seems a natural enough choice for the geographical centre of London. But in the fourteenth century neither the centre of London, nor any part of it, lay here. There was only a village, in which Edward I had put up the last of twelve crosses in memory of Eleanor, his Queen. (This cross was destroyed in 1647. The one now standing is a nineteenth-century reconstruction.)

Eleanor had died in Nottinghamshire and the crosses commemorated the places where the funeral party had stopped on their way to Westminster Abbey. 'Charing' was at one time thought to be derived from the two French words 'chère reine'—dear queen, but it is now known that the place had acquired its name before Queen Eleanor's body rested there.

21

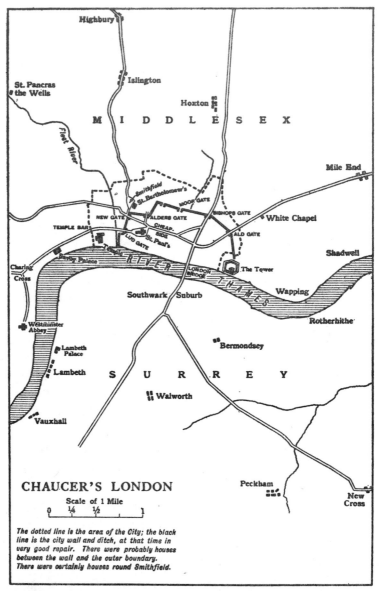

CHAUCER'S LONDON

Scale of 1 Mile

0   ¼   ½   1

*The dotted line is the area of the City; the black
line is the city wall and ditch, at that time in
very good repair. There were probably houses
between the wall and the outer boundary.
There were certainly houses round Smithfield.*

From *English Social History*, by G. M. Trevelyan (Longmans, Green)

London lay one mile to the east of Charing—the length of the modern Strand and Fleet Street. The Embankment is modern. Where we now walk or sit in the gardens, listening to the band, boats used to pull in towards the water-gates of noblemen's houses. The Savoy Hotel stands on the site of the Savoy Palace. In 1357 King John of France was brought there as a prisoner after the battle of Poitiers. Later it was the home of John of Gaunt, who befriended Chaucer (they were the same age—both born in 1340). Gaunt, as pictured by Shakespeare, loved England and spoke of:

> *This happy breed of men, this little world,*
> *This precious stone set in the silver sea . . .*

But England did not love Gaunt. When Wat Tyler and his men marched to London in 1381, they burnt the Savoy Palace to the ground.

Further east, but still not in London, stood the Temple. It was not a temple and never has been. It was an estate, originally occupied by the Knights Templars, who took their name from the Temple of Solomon in Jerusalem. They built circular churches, one of which still stands, restored after bomb damage, to remind us of its founders, as it reminded the fourteenth century. For the Templars had been dissolved in 1312 and their property soon began to be occupied by lawyers, who are still in possession.

The Templars, at the time of their dissolution, were no longer a body of fighting men. The crusades were over. The so-called Knights lived a strict religious life; but they were unlucky. The other religious orders survived in England till the time of Henry VIII. For instance the Black Friars (see p. 91), now commemorated by a bridge over the Thames and a station on the Underground, had reason for considerable satisfaction in the early years of the fourteeth century. Their community lived on a piece of land outside the city wall, at the point where the River Fleet joined the Thames. The wall had now been rebuilt in such a way that the buildings occupied by the friars were safely on the inside of it. The citizens of London, reluctantly, had paid for this improvement.

Fourteenth-century London

London in the fourteenth century was walled, except where the Thames protected it. Below the walls, like a castle's moat, flowed the Fleet and the Walbrook (now both covered in). The line of the wall had remained the same since Roman times. Much of it still rested on foundations which Roman soldiers had laid. In the Roman manner it had round bastions every 250 feet. The wall was twenty-two feet high and at intervals along it there were towers rising to forty feet. Its length —roughly two miles—was pierced by seven gates, all commemorated on the map of modern London. Starting from the south-west corner, i.e. near Blackfriars, there were Ludgate, Newgate, Aldersgate, Cripplegate, Moorgate, Bishopsgate and Aldgate. 'Gate' means not only the gate itself, but also the considerable building which housed it. Newgate and Ludgate contained prisons. Other gates could be rented as dwelling-houses. Chaucer lived in Aldgate for a time.

The eighth gate of London has left no trace on modern maps. This was the gate which guarded the southern end of London Bridge. Perhaps it deserves to be ignored by the namers of streets, since its memory is unsavoury. The custom of decorating it with the heads of men condemned for treachery began in the four-teenth century. The first head belonged to the Scots patriot William Wallace, executed in 1305. (The four quarters of his body were sent to Newcastle, Berwick, Perth and Aberdeen.)

The bridge itself with its nineteen arches and a draw-bridge, was already two hundred years old. A chapel and wooden dwelling houses had been built upon it (the rents of the houses helped to pay for repairing the bridge). In the water below, fish swam. They were caught in nets, but the mesh of the nets had to be wide enough to allow small fish to escape. Two inches at least between the knots was the rule. If you were caught using a narrower mesh, your net was burnt.

Fish throve in the Thames water but Londoners liked something clearer to drink. The Thames, after all, carried the refuse of hundreds of river craft and sea-going ships, in addition to much unauthorized sewage from houses. There were springs and wells within the city, but a further supply was needed. This was found in the country west of the city. There were springs near where Selfridges now stands. Water from these was carried by lead pipes to a cistern in Cheapside—Chepe, as it was then called. 'Chepe' or 'cheap' meant a market. Our adjective 'cheap' is the same word.

Cheapside and St. Paul's

Cheapside was the centre of London—a broad open space where buying and selling and making and mending went on. Nowadays there is a clear difference between the stalls of a market, which disappear at the end of the day, and the permanent, glass-windowed shop; but Chepe contained all sorts of premises from simple fish or vegetable stands to wood-framed merchants' houses three or four stories high, carved and brightly painted. If the weather was fine the wooden shutters of the ground floor windows could be lowered to a horizontal position to make a counter over which business was conducted. There were no glass display windows. Such glass as was then available consisted of small pieces joined by strips of lead (the method still used for stained glass). A window made in this way was very expensive and though it let through the light it was too rough to provide a clear view.

Above the western end of Cheapside towered old St Paul's. Like Wren's cathedral, which replaced it after the Great Fire of 1666, old St Paul's dwarfed every other building in the city and delighted approaching travellers when they saw it first from far away. Then as now, on a bright day, gold flashed from the summit. Then as now an enquiring and energetic person who was ready to climb high could astonish himself with a close-up view of the source of this brilliance—a huge gilded cross.

Today the top of the cross is 365 feet above the street. Its size when, breathlessly, you reach it, is amazing, but you feel that the huge dome can carry the weight. Old St Paul's, on the other hand, had a spire, so that the position of its cross and ball was precarious. At the beginning of the fourteenth century Londoners realized this. They rebuilt the spire, using wood covered with lead. (The spire is the cone-shaped part on top of the tower. Tower and spire together are a 'steeple'.) The new golden ball on the summit was three feet in diameter; the cross above it was fifteen and a half feet high. Inside the cross were holy relics—a stone from Our Lord's sepulchre, bones of the saints and suchlike —put there to keep the spire safe from storms, which it did in fact withstand for over two hundred years.

There was nothing incongruous about giving such a proud position, high above the city, to these holy bones and stones. The London which they overlooked was a city of churches and religious houses, all with relics which the faithful might look upon to give them courage. And 'the faithful' means everybody. As we shall see (Chapter IV), plenty of people laughed or cursed at monks and friars, but no one could cut himself off from the Church. There were churches and religious houses everywhere within the city walls and some outside them too. Outside, for instance, stood St Bartholomew's and St Thomas's, two small religious communities which were already caring for the sick and are now great London hospitals. St Thomas's has moved from Southwark to Lambeth but St Bartholomew's is still on the same site, near Smithfield meat market.

The Tower of London

The only considerable non-religious building in the city which might have caught your eye, as you looked down from the steeple of old St. Paul's, was the Tower of London, and that, although it formed the south-eastern section of the city's defences, was not, strictly speaking, part of the City of London, since it belonged to the King. The Mayor had no authority over it.

From the outside the Tower looked much as it does today, except that there was water in the moat. Its function however has changed. In Chaucer's time it was used to house distinguished prisoners and animals. Examples of the latter were a lion, a lioness, a leopard and two wild cats, presented by Edward III. In the previous century Henry III had kept an elephant.

The Tower also housed one of the Royal Mints (there were others, at Newcastle, Kingston-upon-Hull, Canterbury, Bristol and Exeter). The silver coins (copper was not used) were the groat (4d), penny, halfpenny

and farthing. Edward III added gold coins in 1351—
a noble (6s 8d), half noble and quarter noble.

It is difficult to compare fourteenth-century prices
with today's, but it is interesting to compare them with
each other. Whenever a sum of money—usually a price
or a wage, is mentioned in this book the purpose is to
enable you to compare it with other wages or prices
current about the same time. For instance, to be told
that the controlled price for roast rabbit in a London
cook-shop (a shop from which food was bought ready
cooked) during 1378 was 4d is not very interesting. It
does not mean that rabbit was fantastically cheap. The
value of money was quite different. On the other hand,
if you take a list of prices:

Best roast hen	4d
Best roast pullet	$2\frac{1}{2}$d
Three roast pigeons	$2\frac{1}{2}$d
Three roast thrushes	2d
Best roast pheasant	1/1d
Ten eggs	1d

you can compare the differences between the prices with
the differences between prices in present-day shops;
you can see whether pigeons are still one third of the
price of pullets or whether forty eggs still cost the same
as a chicken.

It is perhaps easy to forget that the existence of
Royal Mints and the fact that minting money was a
royal prerogative (i.e. only the King might have it

done) did not necessarily mean that the King was rich. The Edwards were great borrowers. Earlier Kings had borrowed from Jews, but the Jews had been banished from England by Edward I. They did not return till Cromwell's time. Meanwhile there was no lack of rich Gentiles. There were houses in the city big enough and fine enough for their owners to ask the King to dinner.

A cripple

One of these was Sir Richard ('Dick') Whittington (c. 1358-1423). There is more about him in Chapter V.

The King and his company made a fine show when he came to London. This kind of show was welcome. There were professional entertainers (Chapter VII) but people depended a great deal for amusement on whatever went on in the streets. Grandees by their display and criminals by the variety and discomfort of the punishments publicly inflicted on them, were performing a public service.

30

Rights and duties

So, as a spectacle, the King was welcome; but nobody wanted him to remain in London. The whole point of being a city or borough was to have less interference from the King or the great nobles. London and the other cities of England consisted of large groups of

A blind man and his dog

people who had bought from the King the right to manage their own affairs under an elected mayor and aldermen. This right, which was explained at great length in Latin on a piece of parchment and called a charter, was highly prized. Rights, however, carry duties with them and quite a number of the duties done by a modern town council were already the re-

31

sponsibility of the Mayor and Aldermen of fourteenth-century London. For example:

1. They paved the streets. The paving, which had originally been done by the citizens themselves or their servants, had become an expert job done by 'paviors' at a wage fixed by law. They used cobbles and sand. (Cobbles, which are water-worn, rounded stones, can still be seen in some old towns.) When potholes appeared, the street was not necessarily re-paved immediately. The hole was simply filled with bundles of broom and wood chips.

2. They tried to keep the streets clean. Regulations were made forbidding the throwing of dirty water and rubbish out of windows—penalty 2s (i.e. the value of six roast hens—see p. 29). For putting rubbish in front of a neighbour's door, the penalty was double. Pigs and geese found wandering in the streets were to be caught and sold without recompense to the owner. (London was much less built over then. Many houses had orchards and gardens.)

3. In dry summers they gave orders that a large vessel of water was to be kept in front of every house in case of fire. Ladders were also to be kept ready, and hooks for pulling down burning buildings to prevent flames spreading.

4. They saw to it that, on the ringing of curfew, the city gates were shut and everyone was indoors or able to give a good reason for still being on the streets.

III Inside the Bredon tithe barn

Priest's House, Alfriston, before restoration

The great hall at Penshurst, showing screens and central fire

IV Clock from Wells Cathedral, made in 1392, now in the Science Museum.

The clock at Wells itself is also worth seeing. The oldest clock mechanism in England (1386) can be seen at Salisbury Cathedral.

5. They tried to deal with the smoke nuisance. At the beginning of the century certain tradesmen who used furnaces, e.g. brewers and dyers, found that coal, which was now coming by sea from Newcastle, suited them better than wood or charcoal. But the citizens objected to the smoky fumes given out by the new fuel and forbade its use.

It was one thing to make a regulation and another to see that it was kept—in a city of 35,000 inhabitants with no police force. Complaints of filthy streets continued until the nineteenth century. Complaints about smoke are with us still.

There was supposed to be a guard of about twenty armed citizens on each of the city's gates at night, but how many turned up? It is difficult to imagine Aldgate being as desirable a residence as Chaucer apparently found it, if the clatter of this disgruntled platoon rose nightly from the street below.

During the day, however, the gates stood open. Let us therefore ride out through Aldgate and take a quick look at fourteenth-century England.

Fourteenth-century England

At the beginning of the fourteenth century there were about two million people and eight million sheep in England. The north and west, i.e. that part lying beyond an imaginary line drawn from York to Exeter, was thinly populated. Most of the life of England was in the midlands, the east and the south. Even here,

c

however, there was plenty of room, compared with the situation today (about forty-four million people and fourteen and a half million sheep in England and Wales).

Travel

Some kind of road system, partly inherited from the Romans, linked the country together. There is no doubt that the roads, like the smells of the time, were bad. Many of them were simply tracks, worn by the traffic. Nevertheless, plenty of traffic—pack-horses, carts, foot passengers and horsemen—managed to pass along them. The armies of the Edwards with their accompanying columns of loaded wagons could move across the country to Scotland or to Wales. Queen Eleanor's funeral procession traversed half England on its way from Nottinghamshire to Charing and Westminster. None of Chaucer's pilgrims complains of the state of the road between London and Canterbury. The road from London to Winchester was repaired by William of Wykeham, at his own expense.

The only travellers to whom pity should perhaps be extended are those ladies who had to journey in covered wagons. Coaches, with their shock-absorbing system of suspension, were not invented until two hundred years later. No amount of money could purchase freedom from bumps. Ladies of spirit, unless they were ill, must have preferred to ride, like the Prioress and the Wife of Bath in Chaucer's company.

34

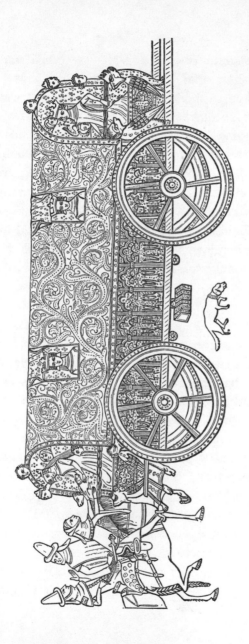

Wagon for ladies

For a man to ride in a cart was considered disgraceful, since that was the way criminals were usually taken to the gallows. For instance, it was related in the *Romance of King Arthur,* that Sir Lancelot, when hurrying to rescue Queen Guinivere, lost his horse. Meeting a carter he seized his cart, because the weight of his armour prevented him walking. When the ladies in their castle saw him approach one said, 'I suppose that he rideth to hanging'.

Queen Guinivere, however, saw by his shield that it was Sir Lancelot, and was angry with the ladies. But it was obviously thought to be a quite natural mistake.

Bridges

The state of the roads probably varied a great deal, but where a river had to be crossed and was not fordable, there had to be a bridge. Paying for this was always a problem. Some bridges were built and maintained by towns, who profited by the travellers and traders they attracted. In the country private charity helped. Instead of just leaving money for a 'chantry', a chapel with a priest, it was possible to have the chantry built on a bridge. On land belonging to the Church an 'indulgence' (remission of penance, see p. 93) could be granted in exchange for work on a bridge or a money contribution. Sometimes the King helped to maintain a bridge either with money or in kind. For instance, three oak trees from Windsor Forest were granted yearly for the repair of the bridge at Maidenhead, on the Thames.

By the fourteenth century many bridges were being built of stone. Some can still be seen, e.g. Redcot Bridge and New Bridge on the Thames above Oxford; Brad-ford-on-Avon, Wiltshire (with a small building for prayer); Wakefield Bridge, Yorkshire (Plate II—it was built in 1342 and has a chapel in the middle where Sunday School is still held at 2.30 p.m.); Warkworth Bridge, Northumberland (with a defensive gateway).

These bridges, however, are better cared for now than they were in the fourteenth century when, for example, the Tweed Bridge at Berwick was unusable for forty years and had to be replaced by a ferry.

Rivers, however, must not be thought of only as obstacles to be forded or bridged. In Chaucer's England they were important highways for the transport of goods and passengers. York, for instance, was an important harbour. The River Ouse was tidal to eight miles above the city.

Towns

How did one find one's way? Not, as a rule, by using a map. Few existed and those few were crude. Part of one, the Gough map, is reproduced on one endpaper and on p. 41, and a diagram based on it is on p. 38. This diagram gives a general impression of the towns and roads of fourteenth-century England. York (11,000 inhabitants) was the largest after London, followed by Bristol, Coventry and Plymouth (which the map has left out). Norwich, Chester, Gloucester and Lincoln, successors of Roman garrison towns, were

From *Historical Geography of England before 1800* ed. H. C. Darby (Cambridge University Press).

also important. The mapmaker has shown the walls which by now surrounded most towns. The other prominent features were, as in London, a cathedral, a castle (where the King could stay and prisoners could

38

be kept), religious houses and, if there was a river, a bridge. The bridge often had a chapel and other buildings built upon it.

Chester is the only town whose walls are still complete, but many gates and stretches of wall remain. York has good examples (Plate II). Newcastle, another important town omitted by the mapmaker, had walls of about the same length as London's (two miles) and a bridge with many houses on it. The 'New' castle, built after the Norman invasion, had long since been replaced by a much more solid building, the central part of which still stands (you can see it from the train on the way to Scotland).

None of these towns was planned. They grew. But town planning was not unknown. In the previous century Winchelsea was destroyed by the encroachment of the sea and Edward I had a new town laid out. He also had a number of new towns built in France, e.g. Libourne on the River Dordogne, called after Leyburn in Yorkshire.

The sea coast

Mysteriously, the mapmaker has omitted the main south-east road out of London, the Roman Watling Street, used by Chaucer's pilgrims on their way to Canterbury and by travellers crossing the Channel from Dover.

Dover did very well out of the traffic to the Continent. Other ports lived on fishing, coastal trade, trade with the Continent and the Mediterranean and piracy. America was not yet discovered, nor had Vasco da Gama rounded the Cape of Good Hope. Ships were small and the steering oar was only beginning to be replaced by the rudder. The mariner's compass was new to this country. It is thought to have come into use in English ships during the fourteenth century. Chaucer mentions it when teaching his son how to use the astrolabe (p. 66).

Southampton was the most important south coast port. The chief import was wine, the chief export wool; but there were plenty of other cargoes—tin, fish and slates from Cornwall, ropes and sails from Bridport in Dorset, wheat, malt and iron from Sussex and Kent.

Wine and wool were important to Bristol but there was also a flourishing trade with southern Ireland, whence came herring, cod, salmon, horses, hides, timber, flax and linen. Gloucester was also a port, though smaller. Her heavy manufactures—nails, horseshoes and weapons of war, could conveniently be moved down the Severn to the sea. Further north Chester was the chief port for Irish trade (Liverpool was not yet important).

On the eastern side of England London dwarfed all other ports and again wool and cloth were the most important exports. Of the south-eastern ports (known as the Cinque Ports, although there were more than five) Hastings, Rye, Romney and Hythe were already losing their importance; but Sandwich was still a good har-

bour. So were Boston (Lincolnshire) and York. Newcastle's overseas coal trade was just beginning. Coal
from there was first exported to France in 1325.

The countryside

All this talk of great walled cities, busy roads and
thriving ports must not be allowed to obscure the fact
that the vast majority of Englishmen still lived and
worked in the country, growing corn and vegetables
and looking after the prime source of English prosper-
ity, which was the wool on the backs of the sheep.
Some of these countrymen were much more prosperous
than others and had bought freedom from the services
due to their feudal lords; but most of them (about half
the total population of England) were still serfs (pp.
103-6).

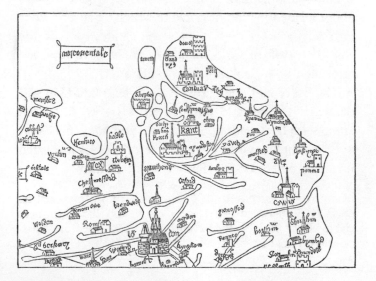

CHAPTER II

AT HOME

Houses in the country

THE NATIONAL TRUST now owns about a thousand properties. Its oak-leaf emblem marks moors and mountains, cliffs and woods, castles and cottages, bridges and barns. But it started through the enthusiasm of two men and a woman and the purchase, in 1896, of the Clergy House at Alfriston, Sussex. This small house was built about 1350. So it is still possible today to walk about inside the kind of home to which Chaucer's Poor Parson, or the Franklin (a small landowner) or the Reeve (a kind of farm manager) might have returned after their outing to Canterbury (Plate III).

The list of National Trust Properties is bound in stiff dark green paper and costs 2s 6d. Write to 42 Queen Anne's Gate, London, S.W.1; or you may find that your local library has a copy. The properties are listed under counties. Under 'Sussex' you will find:

ALFRISTON CLERGY HOUSE. 4 miles NE. of Seaford, just E. of B.2108, between Alfriston church and the Cuckmere river. Bus 98 (Seaford-Hailsham); 126 (Seaford-Eastbourne); [183 : 521029].

'B.2108' is the road number. '183' is the sheet of the inch-to-a-mile Ordnance Survey map on which Alfriston appears. '521029' is the map reference. Having found Alfriston you will see that it has a Youth Hostel (indicated by the letter 'Y'). So you can stay the night. You may want to. It is a lovely village on the South Downs.

The Priest's House is a 'half-timbered' building, which means that it is built on a wooden framework. The roof is thatched and the walls must originally have been of lath (thin wooden strips) and plaster. Bricks were not manufactured in England until the fifteenth century and though some were imported earlier they would have been beyond the means of a parish priest. A stone house would also have been too expensive.

The central part of the house consists simply of one large room, the 'hall'. It takes the whole height of the building. You can look straight up at the beams, blackened by the smoke which found its way from the hearth in the middle of the floor and through a hole in the thatch. Thus the house had no upper story, but the kitchen, at one end of the hall, and the storeroom at the other both had rooms above them.

The priest's 'windows' were almost certainly what we would call 'shutters'. Glass was still a rare luxury in dwelling houses. Yet the priest's rather primitive quarters were much more comfortable than what most country people had to put up with. In Worcestershire you can find:

BREDON TITHE BARN. 3 miles NE. of Tewkesbury, just N. of B4080. Bus X 74 (Birmingham-Worcester-Pershore-Cheltenham); [143 or 144 : 919369]. A fourteenth-century barn, 132 feet long.

Such a building might have housed a peasant's family as well as his animals and his hay. Most peasants however lived in hovels—one example, Teapot Hall in Lincolnshire, survived till 1945. Note 'Hall'. This is not irony. The 'hall' was the main room of any home, however humble and since there was often only one room of any consequence the word was used of the whole house.

In the *Canterbury Tale* told by the Nun's Priest the poor widow had two rooms for herself and two daughters—a 'bour' or inner room, where they slept and a 'halle'. Both are described as 'sooty'. Outside there was a yard fenced with sticks where lived three sows, three cows, a sheep called Malle (Molly), Chanticleer the cock and his wives. The larger animals may have spent the nights outside, but Chanticleer and his wives had a perch in the 'halle'.

At Penshurst, near Tonbridge in Kent, you can see how a wealthy man could provide for himself when he settled down in the country. The great hall (Plate III), now surrounded by later building, was begun about 1340 by John de Poultney, a wool merchant who was four times Mayor of London. The size of the hall is impressive. It is of stone, with a timber roof, but the plan is not so very different from that of the Priest's

44

House. The hall was the only good-sized room in the house. There were only a few small rooms at the end of it. One of these was the 'solar', a sitting-room in which the family could enjoy some privacy. At Pens-

Chimney, Motcombe, Dorset

hurst, as in the Priest's House, the smoke of the fire in the middle of the hall escaped through the roof. Smaller rooms, however, had fireplaces and chimneys. There is one such fireplace in a room in the thickness of the castle wall at Newcastle. Here, it is thought, the

Edwards may have warmed themselves as they passed to and fro on their Scottish campaigns.

Haddon Hall in Derbyshire contains buildings dating

Fireplace, Old Deanery, Lincoln

from Norman times to the twentieth century, but here, as at Penshurst, you can see a fourteenth-century hall. Berkeley Castle (p. 11) also has one. The halls in Oxford and Cambridge colleges are of the same pattern. They have a dais for the high table at one end and, at the other, screens, i.e. a wooden passage with a musicians' gallery above.

Before the days of science fiction there was a type of mystery story in which the more bloodcurdling events took place in a 'moated grange'. A grange meant originally a place where grain was kept; then it came to mean the place where the owner of the grain lived, a country gentleman's residence. Some country houses were protected by a moat. Hence the term, 'moated grange' or 'moated manor'.

If you would like to see a fourteenth-century 'moated grange', go to Ightham Mote, near Sevenoaks (Kent), or to Broughton Castle, Oxfordshire. There is no rigid distinction between a moated grange and a small castle.

Another, less common, type of country house was the tower, with rooms built one on top of the other and reached by an outside stair. Little Wenham Hall, Ipswich, is an example. It also shows that bricks were occasionally used at this time. They were probably brought over from Flanders.

One final word about these country houses. Find out the opening times before planning a visit. A number of houses are not open to the public all the year round.

Houses in town

The large 'hall' type of house could be built as well in a town as in the country, but smaller town houses were nearer to the 'tower' type. Considerations of space made it necessary for them to be built on several stories, with the higher projecting over the lower until the top-most came close to the top story of the house on the other side of the street. They were built of wood though sometimes the roof was tiled. There was a staircase at the back. The ground floor was usually a shop or work-room with a horizontal shutter opening to form a counter as is described on p. 26. Below, there might be cellars.

Each house was not necessarily owned by one person. You could buy a flat (as you can today in Scotland or France, but only occasionally in England). There were constant disputes about who was responsible for doing which repairs, in addition to the usual disadvantages of being divided from your neighbour by only a thin floor or partition. (Evidence for the thinness is provided by the fact that burglars sometimes got in through the wall rather than through the window.)

In these middle-class town houses fireplaces and chimneys were not usual. Charcoal was often burned instead of wood. It is less smoky. The coal referred to as causing a nuisance on p. 33 was not being burned in dwelling houses. Coal was only used as domestic fuel in the districts where it was mined (e.g. in the monasteries near the Tyne).

Not even the biggest houses had piped water or water closets. Wealthier people had baths in wooden tubs, in their bedrooms. Monasteries, castles and manor houses had built-in latrines, often discharging into a river or moat. These latrines are sometimes referred to, e.g. in

Interior of Tower with four latrines on each of three floors, Langley Castle, Northumberland. Section on right shows drainage.

D

A lady bathing.

guide-books, as 'privy chambers' or 'garderobes'. 'Lavatory', when used in connection with fourteenth-century buildings, means a place or a receptacle for washing.

A bath

For instance a basin supplied from a lead cistern was sometimes built into the wall behind the 'screens', so that those entering the hall could wash before eating.

At Home

'Wardrobe' at this time means not a piece of furniture but a good-sized room, sometimes with a fireplace, where clothes were kept.

Furnishings

In *The Book of the Knight of La Tour Landry* (see p. 132), published in 1371, three ladies are described as sitting in a private room when they discover, in the course of conversation, that the same knight has been making love to all three of them. They summon him.

And when he came he said, 'My ladies, what would ye?' and they bade him sit down on the ground by them. And he said, 'Since I am come and must sit, let me have some cushion or a stool, for I might, if I sat low, break some of my points.' So they granted him a stool.

Then they began to question him. But we are not here concerned with his excuses. The passage is quoted to show the lack of chairs and the state of the floor.

It is known that rushes were used as a floor covering, particularly on the ground floor, which often consisted simply of the soil on which the house was built. We also know that these rushes were not so easily come by that one could afford to change them often. Sometimes they stank. But then we come up against the same question which arose over roads and streets (p. 34). Were they all that bad? Was it perhaps a case of some rooms and streets stinking all the time, and all some of the time, but not all, all the time? The above-mentioned knight complained of the risk of breaking

51

some of his points (the tapes which kept up his long stockings); but he raised no objection to the state of the floor. Perhaps on this occasion the rushes were fresh, or it may have been one of the small upstairs rooms with an uncovered wooden floor. The carpeting of floors did not become usual until some centuries later,

Dinner at a trestle table. Only one chair.

but it was not unknown. Edward I's Queen, Eleanor (p. 21), had introduced the custom from her native Spain.

Of the lack of chairs there is no doubt. There might be only one in even a wealthy man's hall. Our phrase 'to take the chair' is now metaphorical, but it originated at a time when the person presiding at a meal or a meeting might really be occupying the only chair available. One of the few surviving pieces of furniture of this period is the Coronation chair in Westminster Abbey. Originally it was brightly painted (Plate VIII).

Tables were formed of boards placed across trestles; hence the expressions 'Board and Lodging' and 'The Coal Board', though now the origin of the word has been forgotten and we talk of a seat 'on' the board instead of 'at' the board. Chaucer wrote of his Knight:

Ful ofte tyme he hadde the bord bigonne

i.e. he had sat in the place of honour. However, the Franklin, the small landowner who went in for lavish entertaining, had 'a table dormant', i.e. a fixed, unremovable table.

Clocks were as yet too cumbersome to be put in private houses and even where there was a clock, e.g. at the Palace of Westminster, at St. Paul's or at Wells Cathedral (Plate IV), it did not have a face. But people were beginning to talk of '—o'clock' as we do now, instead of measuring time by reference to the monastery services, e.g. 'at the hour of tierce' (p. 71).

Boards also served many people as beds. In the malicious story, told by Chaucer's Reeve, about a miller who lived near Cambridge, boards are provided for two visiting undergraduates to sleep on. They had asked for a room for the night, but the miller pointed out with some asperity that he only had the one room in which he and his family lived. Surprisingly, however, he had no difficulty in providing the makeshift bed with blankets and sheets.

Over the beds of well-to-do people canopies projected. These were not simply for ornament. They supported curtains which kept out draughts. Mattresses were of straw, with a featherbed on top when people could afford it. The only other considerable pieces of furniture were cupboards and chests of various sizes in

Bed and cradle

which food, linen, clothes and valuables were stored. Drawers do not appear in English furniture till the following century. Tapestries adorned walls or were hung over doorways to reduce draughts. Some walls had scenes painted on them. A chest is shown in Plate IX.

The metal part of a fireplace now called a grate was then a separate article which could be carried from room to room (like a night watchman's brazier).

They were necessary when coal was burned instead of wood and were therefore mostly found in the north. With them came the poker and tongs which were to remain essential pieces of household equipment until gas, electricity and central heating began to make them superfluous.

In conclusion it must be said that although many museums now have rooms furnished in the styles of different periods you are unlikely to find a fourteenth-century room. Not enough good furniture and fittings have survived. There is a good deal more in France. Their joiners were ahead of ours then.

Food

According to the plan which Chaucer makes the innkeeper of the Tabard put forward, the prize for the best story told during the trip was to be a supper at the Tabard, paid for by the rest of the company. As Chaucer did not fulfil the original scheme of his work and abandoned his pilgrims after he had got them as far as Canterbury, we shall never know the menu of the prize supper. (Supper was the second main meal of the day, taken about five o'clock. The other was dinner, taken about eleven in the morning.)

It is certain however that the Franklin and the Cook would have insisted on the supper being good and the Prioress on its being daintily served. The Franklin, you remember, had 'a table dormant' (p. 53) which was always kept loaded with food. He altered his menus according to the season, but there was always plenty of meat and fish and pies, which he liked served with strong, tasty sauces. His bread, ale and wine were excellent.

The Cook also liked strong flavouring, and in addition to the usual roasting, boiling and frying he made a speciality of 'blankmanger', which was not the 'blancmange' we know, but a savoury dish made by pounding chicken or fish in a mortar with other ingredients. The result was whitish in colour. Hence the name.

The speciality of the Prioress was not cookery but table manners. Nowadays bad table manners arouse comment. Good ones are taken for granted. But under what have been described as 'the ticklish conditions of a fourteenth-century dinner-table'* Chaucer felt the Prioress's delicacy worth mentioning:

> *She leet no morsel from hir lippes falle,*
> *Ne wette hir fyngres in hir sauce depe.*

Nor did she let food drip on to her clothes, and before drinking she wiped her mouth so assiduously that there was not a sign of any grease in her cup after she had drunk. These 'ticklish' conditions consisted in eating without forks and therefore using the fingers a good deal. The only known exception at this period was the fork used by Edward II's unpopular friend Piers Gaveston for eating pears. Utensils were of wood, pewter,

* Eileen Power in *Medieval People* which has chapters on the Prioress ('Madame Eglantine') and on *'The Ménagier's Wife'*.

silver, gold or might be non-existent, according to the means of the eater. A well-laid table was covered with a white cloth and the most prominent object on it was a large salt-cellar.

The gullible carpenter in the Miller's Tale took bread, cheese and a jug of ale as an emergency ration, when persuaded that a second Flood was about to over-whelm mankind. The parish clerk in the same story chewed liquorice to sweeten his breath before making love. The Prioress's dogs were pampered with a diet of roast meat, milk and the best bread. Some cook-shop food is listed on p. 29; but the most varied and sump-tuous menus are those surviving from private banquets. In addition to vast quantities of all the meats eaten to-day including the less common ones such as venison and partridge, the following might be served: heron, crane, hedgehog, peacock, kid, squirrel, porpoise, cormorant, magpie, rook, jackdaw, starling, sparrow and thrush.

Recipes began to be written out in the fourteenth century. The following sauce for serving with chicken or pheasant recalls the modern American habit of serv-ing sweet and savoury together (e.g. ham with pineapple sauce):

Take almonds and pound them, and mix with wine, till they make a thick 'milk', and colour it with saffron, and put it in a saucepan, and put into it a good quantity of figs and currents, and add ground ginger, cloves, galingale [a spice] and cinnamon; let all this boil; add sugar and pour over your bird. [Sugar was still uncommon. Honey was the usual sweetener.]

These ingredients can all be bought today (except for the galingale). Try making the sauce, if you like. But note that you have to make a guess at the quantities and that almonds are likely to be expensive.

There are other more complicated recipes (e.g. To make 'cokagrys': Take an old cock and pull him . . . take a pig and skin him . . . sew them fast together . . . seethe them . . . roast them . . . and before serving, lay gold and silver foil on them); but to the majority of fourteenth-century people such recipes were of no interest, because they could not afford the ingredients. Their problem was not how to cook food, but how to get any food at all, particularly in winter. Like poor people today they lived a great deal on bread and a beverage. Today the beverage is tea. In the fourteenth century it was ale or cider or milk. Chaucer's poor widow (see p. 44) had milk, bacon and sometimes an egg with her brown bread. A sort of stodgy porridge made of meal or beans was a common dish. Meat or fish were rare, particularly in winter. 'A farthing's worth of mussels or a few cockles are a feast for such folk' wrote William Langland in *The Vision of Piers Plowman*.

> '*I have no penny*,' *qoth Piers,* '*pullets to buy; neither geese nor swine.*'

Cheese, curds, cream, oatcakes, loaves made of beans and bran, herbs and cabbage—that was what he and his children lived on.

Monks did better. Their rule against eating meat had

The Abbot's kitchen, Durham

now been relaxed and they usually had other provisions
in plenty (see Chapter IV).

The abbot's kitchen in Durham, built in 1368, can still
be seen. It has four separate fireplaces, each with its
own chimneys.

Clothes

Allas! May man nat seen, as in oure days, the
synful costlewe array of clothynge. . . .

Chaucer's Poor Parson appears in the *Prologue* as
a quiet and wholly admirable person 'in his techying
discreet and benygne'. However, when his turn came to
tell a story, he proved to be something of a fire-eater.
Ignoring the request of the host ('But hasteth yow, the
sonne wole adoun;') he launched into a lengthy sermon which included a detailed examination of the
seven deadly sins. The first of these was Pride. It was
under this heading that the Parson gave his views upon
the fashions of his day. As indicated above, he disapproved of them. In his view people either wore too
much, which was extravagant, or too little, which was
indecent. He was entitled to complain. He objected,
for instance, to one person being enveloped in much
more fur and cloth than was necessary, while many a
poor man had not enough to shield him 'from the dis-
temperance of the firmament'.

However, if one is not considering them from a moral
point of view, the clothes of the fourteenth century are
delightful. It is now for the first time in our history
that women emerge from what one may call the dress-
ing-gown era, the centuries during which the purpose of their clothes had been to hide their bodies.
Henceforth the purpose of women's clothes was to show
off the body to the best advantage. Men too became

60

more elegant in long stockings, which showed the shape of the leg, and pointed shoes. Towards the end of the century women took to shaving their hair in front, so as to produce a broad, high forehead. They also plucked their eyebrows. Such hair as was left after all this was often dyed saffron, and make-up was used on the face.

It has to be remembered, however, that the bulk of the population were little affected by changes in fashion and went on tilling the soil, with scant attention to hair styles, in the same shapeless clothes which their grandparents had worn.

Chaucer is more interested in character than in costume, but (p. 17) he tells us that the Wife of Bath wore red stockings, and in describing Alison, the carpenter's wife in the Miller's Tale he gives a number of details which show that he had looked at the clothes of some women very closely.

Nowadays there is a habit among journalists of describing beautiful women simply by their measurements. This sounds accurate, but Chaucer, without quoting measurements, gave his audience a very clear picture of Alison simply by saying that she was as slender as a weasel ('weasel' in those days meant a small, nimble, carnivorous beast—not a tractor for exploring the polar regions). She wore a white dress with a collar embroidered in black silk and fastened with a big, round brooch, a white gored apron ('gored' means that it was made of several pieces of material, in order to produce a becoming shape), and a girdle of striped silk, from which hung a leather purse adorned with silk tassels. Her hair was tied with a broad ribbon and perched on top of it was a cap with ribbons matching her embroidered collar. She had plucked her black eyebrows to give them an arched appearance and her shoes were laced high up her leg.

She is not stated to have had a handkerchief. There is a tradition that handkerchiefs were only introduced by Richard II, and were therefore not in general use when Chaucer wrote. On the other hand the more refined members of both sexes carried 'kerchiefs'—light silk scarves. They wiped sweat away with them when it was hot, so presumably they wiped their noses with them when it was cold.

CHAPTER III

GROWING UP

Christian and surnames

IF YOU WRITE a play or a story about a particular period, you have to be careful of the names given to the characters. Many of the Christian names of Chaucer's time were not very different from those of today. Here are two lists giving boys' names in order of popularity. The one on the left was compiled from recent birth announcements, the one on the right refers to the time of Chaucer.

Recent	*Chaucer's time*
John	John
David	William
James	Thomas
Charles	Richard
Richard	Robert
William	Henry
Christopher	Nicholas
Simon	Stephen
Mark	Roger
Michael	Simon

Many girls' names known to Chaucer have stood the test of time—Jane, Mary, Elizabeth, Anne, Susan, Barbara, Margaret, Isabel, Frances, Joan. Some have not—e.g. Alditha, Amabillia, Avelina, Roberga, Scolastica, Swanilda.

In Chaucer's time the Christian name was the only one which many children carried throughout their lives. A surname is an additional means of identification and is useful to people who write letters. An educated person like Geoffrey Chaucer, for instance, had a surname, which is thought to be derived from a French word meaning shoemaker. (But even if shoemaking had been the business of his ancestors, it was so no longer. Chaucer's father, as we have seen on p. 13, was a wine-merchant.)

Many of the surnames coming into use in the fourteenth century were from trades, but others referred to the place a man came from (John Francis=John the Frenchman). It was also possible for a nickname to stick and turn into a surname. There were men unlucky enough to be surnamed Godgrom, Piggesfleshe, Weathercock and Gollylolly.

Going to school

Having survived (many babies died) and acquired a name, the average English child of Chaucer's time just grew until it was old enough to help its parents in the fields or in the workshop. A small minority received varying degrees of education, much of it at home or

...ilofe þou þe
ophile first þ mad
a sermoun al þou
of alle þe þingis
þat iesus bigan
for to do ⁊ teche
til in to þe day

in þe whiche iß comaundede to þe
apostlis bi þe hooly goost: who
he chese was taken vp. To whom
⁊ he ȝaue him self aliue oꝛ quic
after his passioun. in many ar
gumentis oꝛ preuyngis bi fourti
dayes: appeeringe to hem ⁊ spekinge
of þe reume of god. And he eetinge
to gydere comaundide to hem þat
þei schulden not departe fro ierusalē
but þei schulden þe abide þe biheeste
of þe fadir þe ȝe herden he seiþ bi
my mouþ. Soþeli iooñ baptizide I
watir: but ȝee schuln be baptisid
in þe hooly goost: not after þes ma
ny daies. Therfore þei camen to gi
dere. axeden him seyinge. Loꝛd: if
in þis tyme: schalt þou restore þe
rewme of iſrael. forsoþe he sei
de to hem. It is not ȝoure for to
haue knowe þe tymes oꝛ momen
tis: þe whiche þe fadir haþ puttid
in his power. But ȝee schuln take
þe vertu of þe hooly goost comynge
fro aboue in to ȝou ⁊ ȝee schuln be
witnessis to me in ierln in al iu
dee and samarie: ⁊ vnto þe vtmeste
of þe erþe. And whanne he hadde
seide þese þingis hem seeȝynge: he
was lifted and a cloude receyuyde
him fro þe eeȝen of hem: whanne
þei biheelden him goynge in to
heuene: loo two men stooden nyȝ
bisides hem in whit cloþis þe
whiche and seiden: men of galilee:
what stonden ȝee byholdinge in
to heuene: þis iesus þat is taken
vp fro ȝou in to heuene: so schal
come as ȝee sawe hi goynge in to

heuene. Than þei turneden aȝen
to ierln fro þe hill þat is clepid
of olyuete þe whiche is bisidis
ierusalem: hauynge þe iourneye
of a saboth. And whanne þei had
den entrid in to þe coupynge place:
þei wenten vp in to þe hiȝer þingis
wher þei dwelten petir ⁊ iooñ ia
mes ⁊ andrew. philip ⁊ thomas.
bartholomew ⁊ mathu iames of
alpheu and symōzelotes: ⁊ iudas
of iames: alle þes weren dwellinge
oꝛ lastynge to gidre in preier wt
wymmen and marie þe moder of ie
su. and wt his breþeren. In þo
daies petur risingeup in þe my
dil of breþeren: seide. forsoþe þer
was a companye of men to gidre: al
meest an hundrid and twenty men
þreuten it biþouȝt þe scripture to
be fulfillid. whiche þe hooly goost
before seide þe mouþ of dauiþ. of
iudas þat was ledere of hem: þat
token iesu þe whiche was noum
brid in vs: ⁊ gat þe sort of þis mi
nystre. And forsoþe þis weldide a
feeld of þe hiyre of wickidnesse and
he haugo to hirte þe middil: and
alle his entrailus ben sched abroad
⁊ it was maad knowen to alle me
dwellinge in ierusalem. so þat þe
ilc feeld was clepid achildruac in
þe langage of hem: þat is to seid
of bloode. fforsoþe it is writ in
þe booke of psalmis. The habita
cioũ of hym be maad desert and
be þer not þat dwelle in it: and
an oþer take þe bischepriche of
hym. þerfore it bihoueþ of þis me
þat maad ben gadrid to gidre wt
vs in alle tyme: in whiche þe loꝛd
iesu entrede in ⁊ wente out amōg
vs bygynnynge fro þe baptisme
of iooñ virto þe day in whiche
he was taken vp fro vs: oon of
þese for to be maad a witnesse

V Page of Wycliffe's Bible, Acts ('Ye Apostles dedes') Ch. I

VI Photo taken in the nave of Winchester Cathedral (built by William of Wykeham) with a cine-camera using a wide angle lens with 143° field.

New College, Oxford, the Cloisters (1386)

Signature of Richard II, aged 19

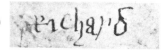

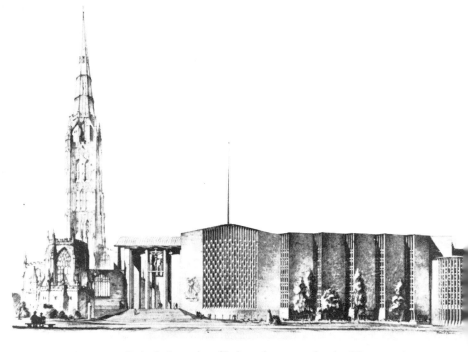

Coventry Cathedral as it will be when completed. The remains of the former cathedral, which was a parish church in the fourteenth century, are on the left

boarding with another family. Such schools as existed were of two kinds, one for younger and one for older children. Those for the younger were called song schools. Singing, reading and writing were taught. The second stage, usually for boys only, was the grammar school—sometimes a boarding school—where only Latin was studied. Both kinds of school were attached to churches, chantries or religious houses. A chantry was a chapel where a priest, paid out of a legacy left by a rich man, prayed for the rich man's soul. But the priest had time for other activities and was glad to earn a little more money by teaching.

A picture of a song school for young children is provided by Chaucer in the tale with which his Prioress entertains her fellow-pilgrims. She describes an unnaturally good boy. This child, aged seven, attended a little school where he was taught singing, reading and good behaviour. He probably learned writing too but not much arithmetic. Even grown-ups did this on an abacus (a counting frame such as young children still use) or with counters.

The language of the songs and reading-matter was Latin and their content was religious. The child learnt to sing 'O Alma Redemptoris' before knowing what it meant, but, when he was told it was a hymn to the Virgin Mary, he determined to learn it by heart for Christmas Day. Before Christmas came, however, he was murdered and his body was hidden in a sewer.

Chaucer may have attended the grammar school

attached to St Paul's Cathedral, which was near his home. Unfortunately he did not leave us a description of his boyhood. We know, however, that he took an interest in the scientific education of his own son, 'little Lewis'. He translated for him from Latin a set of instructions on how to use a navigational instrument called an astrolabe. In the introduction to this translation Chaucer admits that he is not a specialist ('I am but a lewd compilator of the labour of old astrologiens'), but says he has done his best. Modern fathers, growling: 'Why don't the schools start teaching science earlier?', will sympathize.

Froissart's boyhood

John Froissart had a happy childhood. He was born, like Queen Philippa, in Hainault (1338), and later lived for some years at the English Court. It is from his writings that much of our knowledge of fourteenth-century history comes. He was a poet as well as a historian and in one of his poems he lists fifty-two pastimes which he enjoyed as a child, for example—chasing butterflies, hide-and-seek, throwing a feather in to the wind, spinning a top, blowing bubbles, high jump and prisoners' base.

At twelve Froissart went to school. There were some girls at the school; he gave them presents—pins or an apple or a pear. Later a girl gave him three violets and asked him to lend her a book of stories. This put him in a difficulty since books, like all reading-matter before the invention of printing, were a luxury (p. 136). However, he found one, lent it to the girl and was lent one by her in exchange.

It seems that, in spite of the presence of girls, Froissart was at some sort of grammar school, since he says he had to learn Latin and was beaten when he made mistakes. After being beaten, he did better. Out of school he liked fighting. This tore his clothes, so that when he got home he was beaten again; but he got used to this and did not let it spoil his fun.

The decay of French

Froissart was at school on the Continent. Schools, like much else, were similar throughout Western Europe. But England had a language difficulty. This difficulty was not connected with Latin. In England, as in the rest of Europe, Latin was the language of the Church and the language in which laws and official documents were drafted. Educated people could converse in Latin. This was accepted.

Since the Norman conquest, however, French had been the language of the nobility, who presumably expected that it would gradually work its way down through the rest of the population. But this did not happen. On the contrary, English worked its way up. In the second half of the fourteenth century, English became the language of the law courts, schoolboys construed into it and Chaucer wrote in it.

Unfortunately, once English had won the battle,

French did not simply take second place. It ceased to be generally taught. 'Now the children of grammar schools know no more French than their left heel', lamented John Trevisa in the year 1385. His criticism remained true for about five centuries. Only in the last fifty years have serious attempts to remedy the situation been made.

From the parent's point of view

So much for schooling from the point of view of boys and girls. One of the chief worries of parents, however, is—Who pays? The fourteenth-century answer was— Father, or a generous benefactor, or some wealthy person who has left money in his will for educating the poor. There is still in existence the account book of a London merchant who sent his son and another boy, whose guardian he was, to board with the Vicar of Croydon. The boys were heavy on shoes (4d a pair) and stockings (8d or 1s a pair); but the salary of the schoolmaster, whom the vicar engaged, was a comparatively small item. He got 13s 4d a year. It is not surprising that sometimes he had to be presented with a pair of stockings or a coat. The Vicar of Croydon, on the other hand, received less utilitarian presents—a barrel of pickled or smoked herrings, or a small basket of figs.

Another parent whose son was at some sort of boarding school in Oxford, sent a chaplain to see how the boy was getting on. From the chaplain's report, written about 1380, we learn that the boy had brought too many clothes with him. The schoolmaster and his wife asked that in future the boy's outfit should be smaller. The more clothes he brought, the more difficult it was to keep an eye on them and prevent their getting torn. On the other hand the boy was short of books and it was suggested that a selection of extracts from Latin authors, which the owner was offering for 12s, should be bought. The chaplain wrote that he thought the book was worth the money but added that the owner insisted on prompt payment.

William of Wykeham and Winchester College

How many schools of Chaucer's time are still in existence? Very few. Since most of them were attached to religious foundations they were abolished by Henry VIII. Many new schools, independent of religious foundations, were started in the reigns of Edward VI and Elizabeth I. Every year now brings the four hundredth anniversary of a grammar or public school. A few schools however, can claim a continuous history of more than four hundred years. The best known are Eton (fifteenth century) and Winchester.

William of Wykeham, founder of Winchester College and of New College, Oxford, was a poor boy who made good. His name now looks impressive, but all it means is that he came from Wickham in Hampshire. His family was presumably one of the many who had as yet no need of a surname. What sort of people they were is not known.

William was born in 1324. Someone with money noticed him and had him educated in the city of Winchester. His patron must have been a person of influence, since William became secretary to the constable of Winchester castle after leaving school, and, when he was about twenty-three, obtained the first of a long series of appointments in the service of the King. A number of these appointments were connected with building. For instance, Wykeham was Clerk of the Works when Edward had extensive alterations made at Windsor. (A Clerk of the Works was then an administrator, not as now, a man with technical training. See p. 179).

Though he was enthroned as Bishop of Winchester at the age of forty-four, William of Wykeham never studied at the University and was only ordained priest four years before becoming a bishop. John Wycliffe, who was the same age as Wykeham and rose to be a doctor of theology at Oxford, made a sour comment about the promotion of people 'wise in building castles or worldly doing, who could not well read their psalter' and it has been pointed out that Wykeham's collection of books, listed at his death, was small for so wealthy a man. But whatever doubts there may be about Wykeham's intellectual attainments, there are none about his generosity and enthusiasm for education. He founded New College, Oxford in 1379 and Winchester College in 1382.

There were differences between Winchester and

70

other grammar schools of the time. In the first place, it was independent. It was not, like most grammar schools, an offshoot of a larger religious foundation such as a cathedral. This however did not mean that its aims were irreligious. On the contrary, the founder's intention was the provision of better-educated clergy and his college had a chapel.

Winchester's second novel characteristic was its generous endowment and fine buildings. Many of these are still in use and can be visited. They are not spacious or luxurious but they represented an advance. This was probably the first occasion in England when a school was carefully planned and well built. A belfry with a clock was included. Like other clocks of the time (p. 53), it had a striking mechanism but no face.

Thirdly, although the seventy scholars, provided for by the founder, were intended to be poor, they were recruited from different parts of England and in addition a number of boys from wealthy families were admitted. It has been suggested that here, perhaps, is the origin of the English Public School system, although several centuries passed before boarding school education became more usual for rich boys than tuition and service in a wealthy family.

The scholars entered the college between the ages of eight and twelve and many of them proceeded, about the age of eighteen, to New College, Oxford.

Wykeham drew up detailed statutes for Winchester College. These included no provision for the boys to go home for holidays, though they enjoyed a break from work on Holy Days. Free time, however, could not be used for the usual country sports, since dogs, hawks and ferrets were forbidden. The founder also thought it necessary to forbid dancing, wrestling, slinging of stones and throwing of balls in the chapel or the hall; nor might beer be thrown. But no special arrangements for the release of surplus energy were made. There were no regular games or physical exercises. Probably one of the best days for the juniors was December 28th, when they chose their Boy Bishop (p. 144).

Women were entirely excluded, except that a washer-woman, if elderly, might call to collect laundry. Books in the library were not to be sold or given away and, if borrowed for copying, were to be returned on the same day. Long hair, pointed shoes, red shoes or green shoes were forbidden.

Harsh discipline, however, was not part of Wykeham's plan. Only the headmaster might inflict corporal punishment, which was not to be excessive. Other punishments were—being put on short rations or, in the last resort, expulsion.

As a motto for New College, Oxford, Wykeham had chosen the old English proverb: Manners Makyth Man. This also became the motto of his College at Winchester.

Growing Up

Manners

Gilbert Harding's *Book of Manners* includes advice about business correspondence, white lies, behaviour towards foreigners, how to telephone, motoring and difficulties which may arise in connection with public transport. This book came out at the same time as a book about etiquette and a reviewer who had to discuss them both took the opportunity of distinguishing between manners and etiquette. The two overlap, but on the whole 'etiquette' means a set of rules, such as letting a woman go first through a door and not writing 'Mr Smith, Esquire' on an envelope, while 'manners' bring in your feelings—they are shown in the sort of letter you write, or in the way you speak to the telephone operator or in the way you, if you happen to be a telephone operator, speak to the public.

It will be interesting to see whether books about how people should behave to each other will become commoner during the second half of the twentieth century. At present they are far outnumbered by the books which tell grown-ups how to behave towards children. In Chaucer's time, however, it was young women who were thought to be specially in need of advice. *The Ménagier* (i.e. Householder) *of Paris,* was a book written by an elderly Parisian business man for the benefit of his fifteen-year-old wife between 1392 and 1394. The old man took the view that a wife should be as faithful as a dog, who follows his master, wagging his tail, even after a whipping. Humility, however, is not much use without efficiency, so from advice about conduct the author turns to instructions about food and household management. He supplies specimen menus and advice on how to catch fleas, get rid of grease spots and how to look after furs and wine. There are also sections on the management of servants and on gardening. This book appeared too late for Chaucer to have known it well but the picture it presents of what was expected from a young wife is typical of the time. This is not to say that expectations were always realized. Chaucer's character, The Wife of Bath, is anything but submissive.

Female readers may comment at this point that, important though the manners and skills of a young bride may be, it is still more important for a girl to know how to win a husband in the first place. This subject too was not neglected in the fourteenth century and *The Book of the Knight of La Tour Landry* (from which the incident on p. 51 is taken) sought by a succession of stories to illustrate the virtues which would win a husband and the vices that would lose one. There was, for instance, the forward lady who 'waxed right familiar with me for she prayed me two or three times that I should not wait long before coming to see her again . . . and so I said I would not of her, for she was so pert and so light of manners that she caused me to be displeased with her; for which I have thanked God divers times since'.

Growing Up

While the young wife was learning humility, dry cleaning and cookery, her brother, if the family was well-off, might be serving as a page in a great house. There he was partly a maid-servant and partly a soldier. Such was Chaucer's youth. At seventeen he was still making beds and carrying candles, but two years later he saw his first service in France. Note that, like William of Wykeham, he did not go to the University. (Nor did Shakespeare.) At some time however he may have studied law at one of the Inns of Court (p. 78).

Oxford and Cambridge

But plenty of young men (some as young as fourteen) did go to the University, mainly as a preparation for careers in the Church, the law, or, less often, medicine (p.101). As we have seen, scholars from Winchester went up to New College at the age of eighteen, but many boys entered the Universities in their early teens. Several Oxford and Cambridge colleges were founded during the fourteenth century. At Oxford University, Balliol and Merton date from the thirteenth century. To these were added Exeter (1314-16), Oriel (1324), the Queen's College (1341), and New College (1379). The Queen's College owes its name to the fact that it was started by one of Queen Philippa's chaplains.

Like the Paris business man, referred to above, the founders of these colleges laid down the most detailed regulations for their members. At the Queen's College the components of the pottage were specified. Pottage was a stodgy dish, like a very thick soup, which formed the staple food of simpler people. At Queen's it had to be made of beans or peas or a mixture of the two. Wheat or barley was to be added.

So much for the student's inner man; but his outside was not forgotten. Lice were forbidden. Anyone carrying them had his head washed by the college barber.

Queen's was not without traces of its connection with the court. The former royal chaplain ordained that Fellows should be allowed to talk French instead of Latin during dinner, which was announced by a trumpet call. It still is. Here are the notes:*

Colleges however were a new idea. Most students still lived in lodgings. Chaucer's Clerk of Oxenford was perhaps one of these, since he showed no sign of having been nourished on bean and pea pottage, nor did his horse.

> *As lene was his hors as is a rake,*
> *And he was nat right fat, I undertake . . .*

This clerk was a silent bookish person, very different from Nicholas the Spark, the Oxford student who appears in the Miller's Tale. Nicholas dabbled in astrology, played the harp and made love to his landlord's daughter. The discipline of life in a college might have done him good.

* Kindly sent by the Assistant Librarian of the College.

However, the transgressions of Nicholas were mild when compared with the gang warfare in which many students engaged. One day in 1389 a gang 'sought after all Welshmen abiding and studying in Oxford, shooting arrows before them in divers streets and lanes as they went, crying out "war, war war, fle, fle, fle; the Welsh doggys and her whelyps, and ho so loketh out of his house, he shall in good soote [i.e. certainly] be dead;" and certain persons they slew and others they grievously wounded'.

There were also fights between students and townsmen. The bloodiest of these, in which the townsmen were the attackers, began on February 10th 1353 and went on for several days. Many students were killed or wounded and those who could fled from the town. The last of the penalties imposed on the citizens of Oxford as a result of this outrage was only removed in 1854.

The two Cambridge men whom Chaucer mentions were inmates of a college, Solar Hall, which later became part of Trinity. They were northerners with a good sense of humour, who played a leading part in the Reeve's Tale. Colleges, as at Oxford, were becoming a feature of the University. Of those which still exist, Pembroke was founded in 1347, Gonville (now Gonville and Caius) in 1350, Trinity Hall in 1350, Corpus Christi in 1352 and Clare in 1359. The intention of the founders of the last three was to recruit more clergy in order to replace losses suffered in the Black Death.

The Inns of Court

Though law could be studied at Oxford and Cambridge, Londoners did not need to go so far. The fourteenth century saw the growth of the 'Inns of Court', where lawyers lived, worked and received their training. (The legal profession was not yet divided into barristers and solicitors, as it is today). The four Inns which still exist (Lincoln's Inn, Gray's Inn, Inner Temple and Middle Temple) had all begun to develop by Chaucer's time. As we have seen (p. 23) lawyers began to move into the quarters of the Knights Templars when the Order was suppressed in 1312.

Apprentices

In order to enter a skilled trade it was necessary then, as now, to serve an apprenticeship. The usual period was seven years. Apprentices lived with their masters who had complete authority over them. Then, as now, apprenticeship could be the first stage, as in the case of Dick Whittington (p. 98), of a distinguished career; nowadays, however, an exceptionally bright apprentice would probably go on to the university or to a College of Technology, whereas in the fourteenth century he simply pushed ahead in his trade. Another difference between then and now is that today one would not expect to be served by an apprentice in a shop, whereas in the fourteenth century the boy behind the counter very probably was an apprentice. Dick

Whittington, for instance, was apprenticed to a mercer
—a man who dealt in silk.

The fourteenth-century apprentice might envy the
pay packet of his twentieth-century counterpart. He
was not paid, or at least was not supposed to be, though
there are records of small payments to apprentices
being made. Parents who were comfortably off, like
those of Dick Whittington who, despite the pantomime
story, was not a penniless orphan, must have supplied
their apprenticed children with pocket money and
masters could be generous. In 1383 a draper of London
left money to all four of his apprentices. The first got
£5 6s 8d, the second and third £5 and the fourth 10s. If
these sums are compared with other prices in this book
(e.g. p. 136) it will be seen that they were substantial
gifts.

Girls could serve apprenticeships. There is a record
of one Alice, apprenticed to an embroiderer called Elis
Mympe, who ill-treated her. Alice's father made
Mympe pay 13s 4d and release her from the apprenticeship.

'Opus Anglicanum'

The story of Alice is a reminder that, although some
of the English embroidery ('opus Anglicanum') which
was famous throughout Europe in the thirteenth and
early fourteenth centuries, was the work of amateurs—
rich ladies, nuns and monks—much of it was produced
by humbler men and women working for pay.

The word 'embroidery' today suggests tea-cosies and cushion-covers, but 'opus Anglicanum' adorned dignitaries of the Church. Even today a fully-robed Bishop is worth looking at closely, but we should be surprised if we found his cope (i.e. cloak) adorned with action pictures. 'Opus Anglicanum' on the other hand could enrich a cope with pictures of the life of Christ and the martyrdoms of the saints. A garment so gorgeous and interesting invites closer inspection. It has elements of the crude, the beautiful, the comic, the sad, the horrifying and the sublime. It reminds us that we ought not to delay further before proceeding to the next chapter, which deals with the Church, as Chaucer knew it.

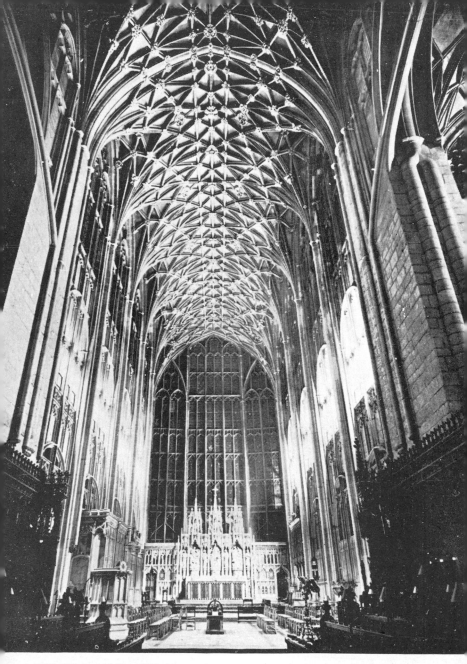

VII Choir and East Window of Gloucester Cathedral (1350). Early example
of Perpendicular style

VIII 14th century door of Pyx Chamber, Westminster Abbey, used as strong-room by Edward III

Coronation Chair, originally brightly painted, made by order of Edward I to contain the Coronation Stone. A similar chair is in the picture on p.52.

Painting in Chaldon Church, Surrey (c1200). Such decorations were common in churches of Chaucer's time, but few now remain. The subject is the Last Judgement. Above are the saved, below are the damned. Bottom right — tree of knowledge and a usurer, sitting on a fire and being attacked by demons with pitchforks. Bottom left — wolf bites toes of girls who danced too much

CHAPTER IV

GOING TO CHURCH

Parish Churches

OLD CHURCHES USUALLY have a list of former Rectors and their dates on the wall. The dates tell you immediately whether the church was there in Chaucer's time, but you can tell by the names alone. There is a point where they become less French. For instance, 'de' no longer appears. This point usually occurs during the second half of the fourteenth century. For instance, at Burnham Deepdale in Norfolk you find

William de Bladington	1344
Nicholas Dockynge	1349
Thomas de Triplowe	1364
John Toke	1385
Richard atte Church	1397

and in Shere, in Surrey you find

Mathew de Redeman	1323
John de Walshe	1331
John de Sancto de Neoto	1364

F

Thomas Cook	1375
Robert Sekyngton	1379
John Walter	1390

Having ascertained whether the church existed in Chaucer's time, you can tell by its style how much of it existed—that is to say, if you know a little about church architecture. If you do not, buy the guide. There is sure to be one on sale for a few pence. Buy it even if you think you can date the various parts of the church unaided. There are sure to be some things which you might miss.

Any Saxon, Norman or Early English work was already old by Chaucer's time. The type of windows which were being built while he was young were mostly in the Decorated style. Perpendicular was beginning (Plate VII) but the most splendid achievements in this style belong to the fifteenth century.

In order to see the church as it was in the fourteenth century you must, in imagination,

(a) Remove

Seating for congregation (extremely rare at this time).

Service books for congregation. (The congregation, most of whom, at least in a country church, could not read, took little active part in the service, apart from joining in the Creed and the Lord's Prayer, both in Latin.)

Organ. (Some churches had organs, but they were small instruments worked by a pair of hand bellows and playing only a few notes. Cathedrals had bigger ones.)

Pulpit (Pulpits existed for outdoor preaching and in cathedrals, but were very unusual in parish churches, where sermons were given from the chancel steps).

Numerous tombs and memorials of later date.

(b) Reinstate

Rood screen of wood or stone, richly carved and painted, between chancel and nave; above it a rood (crucifix) with figures of the Virgin Mary and St John on either side. (Some rood screens survive.)

Paintings, on walls and ceilings, very often showing the Last Judgment and torments of the damned (Plate VIII). (Very few wall paintings survive.)

Embroidery on the priest's robes and on the altar frontal of much greater richness and complexity than is likely to be found today.

Stained glass richer in colour than any but the most modern glass.

The services in this fourteenth-century parish church were Roman Catholic and it is easier to imagine them if you are familiar with the Mass. Masses were said every day and going to church was not confined to Sunday, although it was usual for everyone to go to church on that day. Sometimes a sermon was preached. Some of these sermons were probably very dull. Many priests were ignorant (only a minority went to the University). Books, containing suitable material for sermons, were written but were beyond the means of a poor man; and many priests were poor because part of the money which should have supported them was paid to an absentee (such as William of Wykeham). The sermons of friars (p. 90) were often more interesting. Priests were supposed not to marry but this rule was not strictly enforced.

The priests had to conduct baptisms. The whole baby was dipped in the water. Many old fonts are still in use. The priest also buried the dead. When he married a couple the ceremony began at the church door so that there should be as many witnesses as possible. Church marriages however were not essential. A verbal promise was enough. It has been said that 'the whole world in Chaucer's time was a vaster and more commodious Gretna Green'.*

Manners in Church

Nowadays behaviour in churches is almost always good. Both worshippers and tourists speak quietly, if they have to speak. The only difficulty is over the clothes of women tourists, who are sometimes asked not to wear shorts. (On the Continent there are churches where you can borrow a skirt at the door.)

As we have seen from William of Wykeham's regula-

* G. G. Coulton, *Chaucer and his England.*

tions about red shoes, the fourteenth century was not without its clothing controversies, but they did not arise in church. It was general behaviour—talking and coming in and out during the service—which was lax. Churches were the only public buildings. They were used for meetings as well as worship. People did not associate them with hushed voices and tiptoes.

However, bad behaviour was not confined to ignorant people in small country churches. In Exeter Cathedral, for instance, we find that it extended to the clergy.

The Bishop of Exeter complained in 1330 that certain clergy, during divine service, 'fear not to exercise irreverently and damnably certain disorders, laughings, gigglings, and other breaches of discipline'. For instance, 'those who stand at the upper stalls in the choir, throw drippings from the candles upon the heads or the hair of such as stand at the lower stalls'.

No wonder Wykeham made regulations against wrestling and slinging stones in chapel. It did not however occur, even to his practical mind, to design stalls without 'misericords'. These were tip-up seats with a protuberance (often amusingly carved) on the under side, which propped up the occupant of the stall where he was supposed to be standing. One might have expected a stern disciplinarian to withdraw this support, but Wykeham's New College has fine examples. From our point of view misericords are an excellent idea since the carvers often decorated them with everyday scenes (e.g. husband and wife quarrelling, schoolmaster birching boy).

Rebuilding

Whatever complaints were made about behaviour, the fact remains that churches and cathedrals were full and many had plenty of money for building. The pilgrim was a better source of income than the modern tourist. Becket's shrine at Canterbury (p. 19) was of course the greatest money-maker in the country but there were plenty of other popular tombs. For instance, the possession of Edward II's body brought so much money to Gloucester Cathedral that the choir was rebuilt. Work began towards the middle of the century and the result (Plate VII) is one of the earliest examples of Perpendicular style. Poor, evil Edward therefore made his contribution to England's greatness in the end.

The fourteenth century was not an age of cathedral building as the twelfth and thirteenth had been, but many cathedrals beside Gloucester were improved during the period. For instance, Canterbury, Winchester, Ely, Hereford, Salisbury, Exeter, Norwich, Lincoln, Ripon, St. Albans, Wells, Westminster Abbey and York Minster all contain substantial amounts of fourteenth-century building. York's famous stained glass is from the same period. Chaucer was alive when all this work was going on, but there is no evidence that he saw much of it. He liked London and the Continent.

Going to Church

Monks and Nuns

Having noted that many cathedrals and parish
churches still look very much as they did in Chaucer's
time we have then to remember that hundreds of religious buildings which were whole in Chaucer's time
are now ruins or part of a later building, or non-
existent. These buildings housed communities of monks
or nuns or friars, all of which were later dissolved by
Henry VIII.

There is an admirable map of Monastic Britain in
two sheets published by H.M. Stationery Office. (Your
public library may have a copy.) The various signs on
it make one dizzy. Each represents a religious foundation. Had an aerial survey been made at the time, the
task of interpreting the resultant photographs would
have been comparatively simple. Any big building
which was not a castle or manor house was certain to
be some kind of religious foundation. This general picture was repeated in the towns. In London, for instance,
as noted in Chapter II, if you had looked out from the
steeple of old St Paul's, with its new spire, its gilded
ball and the cross above it filled with holy relics, almost
the only non-religious building within the walls
sufficiently bulky to catch the eye would have been the
Tower of London.

Many of these religious buildings were monasteries
or nunneries. How did they come to be there? Only a
century or two after the Crucifixion there existed,

87

particularly in Alexandria, Christians whom the Christian Church did not satisfy. They felt that as long as they lived ordinary lives in a big city they could not become the kind of people Jesus wanted them to become. So they retired into rocky, deserted places, where they lived alone or in small groups, praying for the salvation of their souls and of mankind. Women as well as men did this. The hard life bred extraordinary gentleness. There are all sorts of stories about the genius of these solitaries for winning the confidence of animals.

In time certain rules were laid down which these early communities of monks or nuns came to accept. These rules insisted on poverty, obedience, chastity and self-mortification (i.e. making yourself very uncomfortable or inflicting pain on yourself). In A.D. 529 St Benedict introduced a new version of these rules into his monastery at Monte Cassino, in southern Italy. Poverty, obedience and chastity were still to be observed but they were to be combined with seven hours' manual labour every day. The daily routine of monastic life was laid down in detail. Furthermore the vows, once taken, were to bind a man for the rest of his life. The rule of St. Benedict came to be adopted in all monasteries and nunneries on the mainland of Europe and was imposed on the monasteries of Britain about A.D. 850.

Did these communities continue to live in poverty, obedience and chastity, insisting that their members did seven hours' manual labour a day?

The short answer is—no. Several reformers tackled the problem and the result was that, by early in the twelfth century, the various 'Orders' had been founded. They existed in Chaucer's time and still exist today, though they number many more members on the Continent than in Britain.

The Orders differed in dress and in minor regulations, but the aim of all was the same—to live in poverty, obedience and chastity according to the rule laid down by St Benedict. (Seven hours physical work a day could not be insisted on when large communities, with divisions of duties, grew up.) The three best-known Orders were the Cluniacs (sometimes called Benedictines because they went on wearing the black dress hitherto worn by all monks and nuns), the Cistercians (who wore white, built their monasteries in lonely places and specialized in agriculture) and the Carthusians (who also wore white, shaved the whole head and lived an even more severe life than the other Orders: they hardly spoke at all and ate only one meal a day).

As with cathedrals, so with religious communities— the men of the fourteenth century had money for those already established but rarely ventured on a new foundation. This may have been partly due to lack of zeal but it was also common sense. The twelfth and thirteenth centuries were 'ages of faith'. The problem for the fourteenth was to keep faith alive within the religious communities which had been founded during the twelfth and thirteenth. The austere Carthusians, however, were an exception to this standstill. The Charterhouse, in London, was founded in 1371 by Sir Walter Manny, a hero of the war in France.

After the Dissolution the Charterhouse became a boys' school and a home for old men. In the nineteenth century the boys' school moved to the country but the old men remained, until their home was burned down as a result of a German air raid in 1941. In 1958 however they were able to return. It is the Elizabethan Charterhouse, not the fourteenth-century monastery, which has been rebuilt; but the line of the monastery walls can still be seen, and as a result of the rebuilding, we have come to know the founder better. Sir Walter Manny's coffin was dug up and revealed the bones of a man five feet seven inches high with an exceptionally broad head, aged about sixty. In all his warring he had broken no bones.

Friars

How would Jesus have wished me to live? What shall I do to save my soul and the souls of all mankind? To these questions the answer of the monks was 'Withdraw from the world'. However, about the year 1200, two men, Francis in Italy and Dominic in Spain, decided that the way to live more like Jesus was not to withdraw from the world, but to go out into it, meet every kind of person and preach the gospel everywhere. This task of guiding, comforting and encouraging ordinary people properly belonged to the parish priest, but that there was need for something more was shown by the immense success of the 'friars' founded by Francis and Dominic and called after them Franciscans and Dominicans.

'Friar' means 'brother'. These men wandered throughout Europe preaching. They depended entirely upon charity, owning nothing but their rough peasant's robe belted with a piece of rope, and their begging bowl.

By Chaucer's time, some two hundred and fifty years later, much of the original idealism of the friars had evaporated and their work had become more comfortable. Many towns had a Grey Friars' (Franciscan) or a Black Friars' (Dominican) establishment. You may remember that the Black Friars of London were powerful enough to get the city wall altered (at the citizens' expense) in order to include their group of buildings (p. 24).

Chaucer's churchmen

What did Chaucer think of the Church?

The first thing which strikes us about the company, which set out from the Tabard Inn, Southwark, in April 1387, is that, numerically, the Church is well represented. Out of a company of about thirty, eleven are clerics and the Canon who joins the company near Canterbury makes twelve. There are also a number of clerical characters in the tales. The general impression of the Church given by these people is not favourable. Only the Parson was concerned with the basic questions—How would Jesus have wanted me to live? How would Jesus have wanted me to advise others? Only the Parson was poor (financially. He was rich, we are told, in holy thought and work).

The highest church dignitary on the pilgrimage is the Prioress, who is escorted by another nun and three priests. She has very good table manners, and an attractive name—Madame Eglentyne. She is neatly dressed. Her golden brooch is inscribed with the words 'Amor vincit omnia'—'Love conquers all'. But love of what? Dogs? Madame Eglentyne loved dogs.

At this the reader may ask resentfully whether it is fair to take Chaucer's fictitious characters as representative of the real people of his day. The answer is that, up to a point, it is fair. One cannot of course argue that because Chaucer's Parson was conscientious, the average fourteenth-century parson was conscientious. Nor can one conclude that the average prioress was prim. But Chaucer is not our only source of information about his times and, when all that is known is taken into consideration, it becomes clear that the pilgrims are all people one might have met.

The Monk ignored the rule of St Benedict and was mainly interested in hunting and good food. The Friar was out to make as much money as possible. The Clerk of Oxenford was studious, quiet and, as noted in Chapter III, thin; but these apparently admirable qualities were not thought likely to lead him to a successful career. He was not worldly enough—that was the trouble.

Since the Summoner's occupation was a combination of snooper and law-court official, it is not surprising that he is painted as an unattractive character. He had to bring delinquents before the church courts (p. 163), which dealt with moral offences. Apparently he spent his time trying to catch people kissing and then getting them to offer him a bribe in order that the offence should not be reported. The Pardoner had no need of bribes since he made a good living by selling indulgences—papers issued by the Pope which were supposed to secure indulgence (i.e. less purgatory) for the buyer after he was dead. A big sin needed a big payment.

One of the ways of estimating the truth of Chaucer's portraits of the nun and the monk is to look at the reports made by Bishops whose duty it was to inspect religious houses. Many of these reports survive. They reveal the kind of irregularities which were practised by the Prioress and her like. In the first place she ought never to have been on a pilgrimage. Participation in pilgrimages was forbidden to nuns, which is not surprising, since such expeditions had become more like the firm's annual outing than an act of worship and devotion.

Secondly, the Prioress's dogs were entirely out of order. Reports on nunneries are full of complaints

93

about the breaking of the regulations against keeping pets. In the very year, 1387, in which Chaucer's 'pilgrims' are pictured as setting out, William of Wykeham was writing a stern reproof to the Abbess of Romsey (Hampshire) on just this point.

Remember, though, that in any report of this sort we are likely to hear more about what is wrong than about what is right. We must therefore remind ourselves that plenty of communities were still leading lives which were governed more or less, by the rule of St Benedict. The description of life in a monastery which forms part of history books dealing with the twelfth and thirteenth centuries holds true to some extent for Chaucer's day. The main differences, apart from the spectacularly scandalous behaviour pilloried by Chaucer and confirmed in Bishops' reports, were that accommodation was less austere (abbots in particular were very comfortably housed) meat-eating was generally allowed and monks were given wages for performing their various duties, so that they had money to spare after they had paid for their clothes and other necessaries.

Another difference was that, by Chaucer's time, monasteries were no longer the only centres of learning and the arts. In earlier centuries a monastery had been the only place where the thinking and the manual labour connected with producing a book could be done. (The manual labour was the copying and the production of illustrations.) Now, however, Chaucer could com-

94

bine literary work with life at court or in what corresponded to the Civil Service or with soldiering, and there were plenty of lay craftsmen able to produce exquisitely written, illustrated and bound copies of a manuscript.

In the field of scholarship too the monasteries were now much less important than Oxford and Cambridge. Houses were established at the two Universities where monks could live for a period of study. Only a minority did so. They had to be clever and their monasteries had to pay for them. Similar arrangements were made for friars.

John Wycliffe

John Wycliffe, a Yorkshireman, had the good fortune to be able to live in Oxford at the Queen's College (p. 76) and study theology at his own expense. His income, though incomparably smaller than William of Wykeham's, came partly from the same source— parishes where an ill-paid substitute priest officiated. But good came out of evil. Congregations which never heard a good sermon except from an occasional visiting friar, gradually came to know a new type of salvationist—the Lollard. Lollards—travelling priests— were Wycliffe's creation, though they were more influential after his death (1384) than during his life. They attacked the worldliness and insincerity of the Church, as friars had long ceased to do. Sometimes they brought with them parts of Wycliffe's translation of the Bible.

95

For the first time, men and women heard the Lord's Prayer in their own language:

Oure fadir that art in hevenes, halewid be thi name; thi kyngdoom come to, be thi wille don in erthe as in hevene; gyve to us this dai oure breed . . .; and forgyve to us oure dettis, as we forgyven to oure dettouris; and lede us not into temptacioun, but delyvere us fro yvel. Amen.

CHAPTER V

EARNING A LIVING

CHAUCER'S PILGRIMS CLATTERED out of the Tabard Inn (they all seem to have been mounted, even the humblest, such as the Haberdasher and the Carpetmaker) heading south-east, along what is now A2. Forget about them for a moment and have a look at the road which leaves London for the north, over Highgate Hill. The A1, the Great North Road, now avoids this hill, branching off to the right from Archway Underground station. But the old road over the hill is still much used. You can either walk or take a bus. Halfway up the hill is a stone (Plate IX), surrounded by an iron railing and inscribed:

SIR

RICHARD WHITTINGTON

THRICE LORD MAYOR

OF LONDON

1397—Richard II

1406—Henry IV

1420—Henry V

Dick Whittington

There are three mistakes in this inscription. In the first place it is nowhere recorded that Whittington was knighted. Secondly, the Mayor of London was not yet called Lord Mayor. Thirdly, Whittington was Mayor in 1398, making four times in all. However in comparison with the stories which were later told about Whittington and now reappear annually in Christmas pantomimes, the stone is accurate. Other known facts about Whittington are that he was the third son of a Gloucestershire knight and became a mercer. He left a vast fortune, part of which went towards the foundation of a home for old people which was moved, early in the nineteenth century, to Highgate, where it still is. This is Whittington's only connection with Highgate. His halt on the hill, his hearing Bow bells and his consequent return to London are as legendary as his poverty and his cat.

Whittington's career shows that a fortune could be made in London, but we do not know how he set about making it. We do know, however, that he had two great advantages—he was the son of a knight and he married the daughter of a knight. William of Wykeham is a better example than Whittington of a spectacular rise from poverty to enormous wealth.

Chaucer's merchant

What advice has Chaucer on how to get rich in the fourteenth century? There is a Merchant among his characters. He is easily recognizable in his fine beaver hat and brightly-coloured clothes; his neat forked beard moves up and down as he talks. We hear from him about his successful business deals and his unsuccessful marriage. Chaucer adds the information that, in spite of his appearance, the Merchant was in debt.

The lesson to be learned is that a successful four-teenth-century business man should be well dressed and give a good account of his business life, whether in fact it is going well or not. The only failures he may admit to are in his home life.

How did Chaucer earn his living?

As we have seen (p. 13) Chaucer's father was a business man, in the wine trade; but Chaucer did not take up a business career.

What else could he have done? No one could at that time earn a living as an author. There was no *Careers for Men and Women* series published by a considerate Ministry of Labour and National Service and containing a booklet on *Journalism and Publishing*. No advertisements invited one to cut out and post a coupon in order to receive details of how to write successful short stories. For that matter there was no advertising industry with its opportunities for writers of bright copy in prose or verse. How about teaching or the Civil Service? Teaching was still entirely in the hands of Churchmen; so was most of government administration. But the tendency was for more government posts to be open to laymen and Chaucer did in fact become what we would now call a Civil Servant. Since, however, there was no competitive examination, entry depended on influence. Chaucer had reason to be thankful to his father for giving him an aristocratic education which put him in contact with influential people.

Two other professions which now began to offer opportunities to laymen were the law and medicine.

Lawyers

Lawyers studied at Oxford, Cambridge or the Inns of Court (p. 78). On graduation they received the title of 'Sergeant' and a Sergeant of the Law is one of the less attractive characters in Chaucer's company. Lawyers were as unpopular as millers (p. 112). Two other poets of the time, Langland (p. 104) and Gower, wrote contemptuously of them. Wycliffe denounced them as corrupt oppressors of the poor.

During the rising of 1381 the poor, for a time, revenged themselves. On the whole the rebels only killed unpopular individuals but lawyers were attacked as a class. This class included the judges.

The Chief Justice of England was in Suffolk at the time of the revolt. He had been engaged on the enforcement of the Statute of Labourers (the law of 1351 by which it was hoped to control the rise in wages which resulted from the Black Death). As soon as the rising started, the peasants were out for his blood. He fled. Near Lakenheath, now an enormous bomber station, then a small village, he reached the river. If he crossed the river he might be safe. A boat lay ready by the bank.

Near the boat, however, was a woman. Suddenly the positions of judge and judged were reversed. This woman had it in her power to condemn the Chief Justice of England to death. All she had to do was to push the boat out before the fugitive reached it. This she did. Next day the Chief Justice's head was on view in the market place of Bury St Edmund's. Nor was it alone. Another band of rioters had hunted down the Prior of the abbey. His head too was available. It was stuck up with its lips pressed against those of the Chief Justice as a reminder that these two well-hated men had been allies.

Doctors

There were not many doctors or surgeons (the distinction was not yet precise and much minor surgery was performed by barbers). You would not have found a doctor in every village, as you would have found a priest; and of those who called themselves doctors few had taken a degree in medicine at the University. They were not necessarily the worse for that, since their studies would have been more theoretical than practical. Only at certain Italian universities were medical students able to watch dissections.

Chaucer's Doctor was quite well off. His clothes were lined with taffeta. It may be that Chaucer, when describing him, was thinking of John of Arderne. Arderne was first an army doctor, next practised at Newark (Nottinghamshire) and finally came to London in 1370, where he wrote a book about surgery which contains much sensible advice on how doctors and surgeons should behave. Some of this advice has to do with fees, which were enormous, if the patient was rich enough to pay. Fifty per cent, it was suggested, should be paid in advance. For a certain difficult operation £40, plus a yearly payment thereafter of £5, might be asked.

Chaucer's Doctor shares with John of Arderne an interest in fees and in astrology; but Arderne's book does not suggest that he was a shallow or unpleasant character. The standards of conduct he lays down are those which most of us would like to see followed by our own general practitioner. The doctor, says Arderne, should not boast; he should keep up-to-date by reading; he should not get drunk; he should not express opinions about other doctors; he should not kiss the ladies in great men's houses (kissing was a more usual greeting then than it is now: in the houses of lesser men Arderne apparently sees no objection to it); he should be neatly and soberly dressed (unlike Chaucer's Doctor, who wore scarlet) with clean hands and with nails properly manicured; he should never tell lies (although when asked how long a cure will take he should overestimate the time, so as to be sure of not disappointing the patient); he should have a stock of proverbs to comfort his patients and good stories to amuse them (the

102

Bible is recommended as a source of amusing stories).
Arderne probably means parts of the Old Testament,
chattily retold, as in the Miracle Plays (Chapter VII);
finally he should never betray the secrets of his patients,
or talk slightingly about one of them to another.

All this is excellent advice. Manners and funny
stories have their place in the medical profession. But,
of course, the main question to ask about any doctor is
—Can he make his patients well? When the testing
time came in 1349, during the Black Death (a gold mine
for Chaucer's Doctor and for others too no doubt), the
answer was almost always 'No'. Strong alcohol was
often prescribed. It did not cure the plague but many
patients thus tasted brandy, gin and liqueur for the
first time. By the end of the century they were known
throughout Europe.

Work on the land

In the country, where most people lived, it was not
often much use for a serf to be ambitious. It is not
much use a prisoner being ambitious in jail and the
comparison between a serf and a prisoner is valid, up
to a point. A prisoner's best course is to work hard and
behave himself, unless he can escape with a reasonable
chance of not being recaptured. The chances of better-
ing himself—changing to a pleasanter job or earning
more money—are small. All this was true of the serf,
though it need not therefore be supposed that his lot
was always one of unrelieved misery. He was a kind of

slave (p. 159) and the lives led by slaves whether in ancient Rome or in nineteenth-century America or elsewhere, have always varied in accordance with the characters of their masters. Furthermore a serf could sometimes buy freedom from some or all of his feudal duties.

Take that kindly pair of Canterbury pilgrims, the Ploughman and his brother, the Poor Parson. They would appear to have climbed a little out of the rut. Certainly the Parson had. He was a learned man, although it had not done him any good financially. As to his brother, it should be remembered that 'ploughman' in Chaucer's time simply meant 'countryman' (after all, pretty well everyone in the country had some land and ploughed it) so this 'ploughman' may have been a small tenant farmer who paid a money rent and no longer owed services to his lord.

Piers Plowman

The most famous fourteenth-century 'ploughman' was called Piers. He is a character in a poem which bears his name—*The Vision of Piers Plowman*. This poem resembles the *Pilgrim's Progress* in some ways. It describes a series of dreams or visions. It leaves one with the impression that the writer was deeply worried about the state of the world of his time and had a message of hope not only for his own, but also for later generations. But we know much less about William Langland, the author of *Piers Plowman*, than we know

104

about John Bunyan. Langland was born in the Malvern Hills and grew up in poverty. But he went to school and may have become a priest. He was lanky and not strong; so farm work did not suit him and he found his way to London. He was no pantomime Dick Whittington. He married and had a daughter but they all lived in squalor. Langland went on writing and rewriting his poem. The only money he earned came from saying prayers for rich men. Rich men not only founded chantries where their souls could be prayed for after death; they were also glad to be prayed for during life. Any man with enough sense to make a fortune had also enough sense to realize that the means by which he had acquired it would make him a strong candidate for hell, as soon he was dead.

Huckleberry Finn's remark about the *Pilgrim's Progress*—'The statements was interesting but tough' applies even more to *Piers Plowman*. Piers, although the central figure of the poem, does not appear at all in large sections of it and he changes his identity from that of the ideal, simple, honest, countryman to that of a figure, who, in the poet's mind, is clearly Jesus Christ Himself. Yet from all this emerges a clear picture of the wretchedness of the poor and the corruption of the Church, together with a message of encouragement and hope.

The *Canterbury Tales* are read in schools and set for examinations. Chaucer is buried in Westminster Abbey. *Piers Plowman* is less well known and no one has any idea where Langland is buried. But it was Langland's poems and not Chaucer's which put heart into men like John Ball, as they led the revolt of 1381. If that fight was worth fighting, you may think that the complicated work of this lanky, praying poet was worth the long years of squalor which he devoted to it. Here, from Langland's poem are some of the varied ways in which his contemporaries earned their living:

Barons and burgesses and bondsmen too
I saw in this assembly, as you shall see later,
Bakers and brewers and butchers galore,
Weavers of wool and weavers of linen,
Tailors and tinkers and tax-collectors,
Masons and miners and many other craftsmen,
All kinds of labourers alive, leaping out together,
Such as diggers and ditchers, doing an ill day's work,
Dallying through the long day with a 'Darling, how goes it?'
Cooks and their kitchen-boys calling 'Hot pies!
Good geese and gammon! Get a good dinner!'
Advertising taverners told the same tale
With a 'White Alsatian wine! Red wine of Gascony!
Rhenish and claret give relish to a roast!'

Here is another list of occupations. This time the company is assembled in an ale-house:

Cissy the sempstress sat on a bench,
Robin the rabbit-catcher and his wife with him,
Tim the tinker and two of his apprentices,
Hickey the hackney-man and Hodge the Huckster
. . . Davy the ditcher and a dozen others,
A fiddler, a rat-catcher, a Cheapside crossing sweeper,
A rope-maker, a roadman and Rosy the dishwasher,
Several salesmen of second-hand furniture.*

* Coghill's translation

The Luttrell Psalter

Langland did not illustrate his work with drawings or paintings, so far as we know; neither did Chaucer. But about the year 1340, when Langland was a child and Chaucer a baby, there was an artist at work in East Anglia with whose way of looking at people and things they would have been in sympathy. This artist was a layman. Monks, you may remember, no longer had a monopoly of the skill necessary to produce a handsomely written and illustrated book. There were now uncloistered scribes and illuminators (i.e. illustrators) who could be hired. The hiring in this case was done by Sir Geoffrey Luttrell of Irnham in Lincolnshire (you can see his tomb in the church there). He wanted, and got, a psalter (a book of the Psalms)—full of entertaining pictures. That was the custom of the time. Illustrations in psalters did not have to be connected with the text beside which they appeared. The artist had a pretty free hand. In Sir Geoffrey Luttrell's Psalter this free hand was usefully employed—at any rate from the point of view of posterity. No one knows what Sir Geoffrey thought of this now fabulously valuable work. He did not even mention it in his will, and he made a long will, including ample provision for his friends to eat and drink on the day of his burial.

It was the artist's idea to provide his patron with a mixture of fantastic creatures (some of whom look like a science fiction writer's idea of the inhabitants of

Mars) and ordinary people, like the bagpiper shown on p. 142. Those who are shown performing the yearly cycle of agricultural operations (ploughing, sowing, harrowing and so forth) are often seen. The British Museum have put them on to a series of postcards and few books about the fourteenth century omit them. But to realize fully the immense amount of detailed information about customs and conduct which the Luttrell Psalter contains, it is only necessary to read a section of the index, which has been made for it. Here, for instance, are some of the entries under 'C':

> Cap, winged, worn by executioner
> Cart, country, driven by monkey
> Cart, harvest, driven up-hill
> Cat and mouse,
> Catherine, St
> Cauldrons
> Cherries, boy stealing
> City, medieval (Constantinople)
> Clerks, at a lectern
> Club, spiked
> Christopher, St
> Coffin, stone
> Coif, elderly man wearing
> Confessor-Franciscan
> Cripple, in wheelbarrow

Carpenters

There are several carpenters in the *Canterbury Tales*. There is one among the pilgrims, but he is not described separately. A haberdasher, a dyer, a weaver and a carpet-maker share a slightly contemptuous paragraph with him. These five men looked prosperous and were smartly dressed. Each had a pushing, ambitious wife at home.

The Reeve, an official concerned with estate management who is pictured as skinny, short tempered and sly, turns out later (in the *Prologue* to his own tale) to be a carpenter by trade.

The carpenter of whom we learn most is John, one of the principal characters in the Miller's Tale. He was rich and lived with his wife in a house of at least two stories in which a student lodger had a room of his own. No children are mentioned, but we hear of a maid and an apprentice. This satisfying picture, however, is clouded by John's monumental gullibility. He allows himself to be persuaded that the second Flood is about to descend on mankind and waits for it, asleep in a kneading-trough, which he has slung from the rafters. His sudden and undignified descent from this position is the climax of the story.

So much for John's character. Of his carpentry we hear only that he made the ladders necessary for climbing into the kneading-troughs. But John had probably built his own and many other houses. At a time when only the most important buildings were constructed of stone and bricks were still uncommon, a carpenter was principally a builder. He undertook the whole operation, beginning with the felling of the necessary timber.

Carpenters also made coarse furniture. Better furni-

ture was made by the joiner, i.e. the man who specialized in making neat joints. Nowadays, since most furniture is made in factories, the distinction between carpenters and joiners is disappearing. You will not find the
two trades taught separately in technical schools.

A number of the carpenter's tools were similar to
those still used today. He had hammers, mallets, saws,
chisels and probably a plane, but no screwdriver.
Screws were not generally used until the seventeenth
century. He used wooden pegs or iron nails made by
the blacksmith and drilled holes with gimlets, with
large gimlets called 'augers' and with bit and brace. He
had a level, plumb-line and square. But two tools which
he used a great deal—the axe and the adze (an axe with
the blade at a right angle to the handle) are little used
by carpenters now, because wood comes ready shaped
from the sawmill.

In the fourteenth century a carpenter, having felled
a tree and lopped the branches, had to split the trunk
with axe and wedges or by sawing it into planks, probably with a two-handed saw, which needed two men
to work it. However, machinery to help him was on the
way. The first record of an English sawmill is in 1376.

A usual wage for a carpenter shortly before the
Black Death was 3d a day. After the Black Death, in
spite of the Statute of Labourers (p. 100), it sometimes
rose to 5d or 6d.

Millers

The Miller's story about John the carpenter so exasperated the Reeve (himself a carpenter) that he proceeded to tell a story in which a miller was made a fool of. There are thus two principal millers in the *Canterbury Tales*, the brawny, red-bearded, sly, amateur bagpiper, who took part in the pilgrimage, and the miller of the Reeve's Tale, a man of similar character, shape and hobbies (he played the bagpipes too).

When slavery disappeared with the advance of Christianity (after about A.D. 500) people began to look round for a source of power more efficient than the muscles of men or animals. They found it in water and wind. The first use to which water and windmills were put was the grinding of corn. Soon they were used to help a variety of trades. There were sawmills (see p. 110), fulling mills (these were in fact the earliest washing machines) and mills for crushing iron ore. But because corn-grinding by mills came first, the word 'miller' came to mean a grinder of corn.

Windmills and Water-mills

Far from being a blessing, the corn mills were an additional burden to country people, because the lords of the manor managed to establish a monopoly. No one else might own a mill and all grain had to be ground in the lord's mill (you were even forbidden to do it by hand at home).

Millers were unpopular partly because the forced use of their mills was unpopular, and partly because they made things worse by taking advantage of every opportunity for cheating. It was obviously difficult to check that all one's grain had been ground or that an inferior grain had not been substituted.

A windmill. It can be rotated to face the wind

By the time of Domesday Book (1086) there were thousands of water-mills in England, but it was some time before people realized that wind could also be used to push round a wheel. The first windmills were clumsy, because the whole structure had to be turned to face the wind. It was probably only during Chaucer's lifetime that the tower-mill was introduced. This had a stationary base and only the top revolved, carrying the sails to face the wind.

112

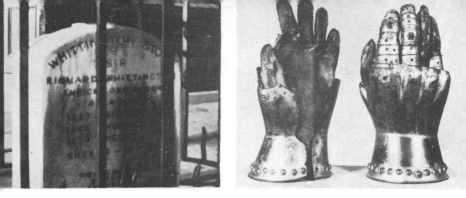

IX Whittington Stone (See p.97)

Gauntlets of the Black Prince. The lining is of buff leather embroidered with silk. They hang above the Prince's tomb at Canterbury (Plate I)

Oak chest made of horizontal boards mortised into four uprights—an example of fourteenth century carpentry.

X The carving of alabaster was a flourishing industry, particularly in the Midlands, from about 1350. Panels between one and two foot high, were used to decorate altars. They were painted and gilded. The above panel (1400) shows the Resurrection. The soldiers wear the dress of the time.

Gilds

Chaucer's group of five artisans—haberdasher, carpenter, weaver, dyer and carpet-maker

> . . . *were clothed alle in o lyveree*
> *Of a solempne and greet fraternitee;*

'O' means one; 'lyveree' means livery, a kind of uniform.

These five men all belonged to the same fraternity or gild. This particular gild seems to have been a club

Forging

of respectable and prosperous men from various occupations; but we hear more often of 'Craft Gilds', associations confined to men, and sometimes women, of one craft.

The Craft Gilds had started as groups in which all the members, when they first entered as apprentices (p. 78), had roughly similar prospects. When they had finished their apprenticeship, they became journeymen; after a number of years as journeymen, they set up as masters.

H

There was a certain amount of comradeship between older and younger members of a Craft Gild; they were united in rivalry against members of other gilds, or craftsmen from another town, or unskilled men.

By Chaucer's time, however, the modern division between employers and employed had begun to appear. As trade increased, differences in success and wealth in-

Grinding

creased. A simple master employing a few journeymen and apprentices clearly could not talk as an equal to men like Whittington, who mixed with the richest and most powerful men in the country. And the success of large-scale organizers and salesmen like Whittington meant not only that small masters were squeezed out; it meant that many journeymen had to face the fact that they would never become masters at all.

Thus a division arose in the Craft Gilds between employers and employed. There were occasional strikes

114

for higher wages within the Gild and in some cases separate 'Yeomen Gilds' were formed by journeymen and small masters. It is these Yeomen Gilds rather than the Craft Gilds which are comparable to the modern Trade Union.

A mixed bag

One of the first of many foreign weavers, whom Edward III allowed to settle in England, was Han-

Wheelbarrow and truck

keinus de Brabant, who came to York in 1336. The word 'hank' (i.e. a skein or coil of wool) is thought to be derived from his name.

Coal was mined in the Tyne valley, tin in Cornwall and iron in Cumberland, but miners were a small and unimportant section of the community. Steel (for armour, weapons and the finer types of tools or instruments) had to be imported.

115

Oxen were still preferred to horses for farm work because they needed less to eat and did not have to be shoed.

Wheelbarrows were in use. They had been invented in the thirteenth century.

The eyes of needles were a form of hook. Needles did not have pierced eyes until the fifteenth century. This however did not affect the standard of embroidery (p. 79).

Price for catching: Old moles 2s a hundred; young moles 1s 3d a hundred; rats ¼d each.

Advice on choosing a career (from *Piers Plowman*):

'Counsel me Kind,' quoth I 'what craft is best to learn?'
'Learn to love', quoth Kind, 'and leave off all other.'
'How shall I come to money so, to clothe me and feed?'
'If thou love loyally,' quoth he, 'lack shalt thou never
Meat nor wordly weed, while thy life lasteth.'*

* Coghill's translation

CHAPTER VI

FIGHTING

IN THE SUMMER of 1346, when Froissart was still a child chasing butterflies in Hainault, the Black Prince, aged sixteen, was fighting his first great battle. This was at Crecy, near the River Somme, in northern France. Later, when he had established himself as a courtier and a writer in England, Froissart was able to talk to men who had fought at Crecy and his account of the battle is contained in one of the earliest chapters in the bulky history which finally ran to four volumes. (Good English abridgments can be bought, but there is no cheap edition of the whole work.)

According to what Froissart's informants told him, there was a moment during the battle when the Black Prince's position became dangerous. The nobles who where fighting beside the Prince sent a messenger back to the King, who was commanding the battle from a position in the rear beside a windmill. He could get a good view from there.

The messenger explained the position and asked that help should be sent. The King asked:

'Is my son dead, or so badly wounded that he cannot help himself?'

'No sir,' said the messenger, 'but he is hard pressed and needs your help.'

'Go back,' answered the King. 'Tell them not to send for me again as long as my son is alive. I will not come. I want the boy to win his spurs.'

This message put heart into those fighting around the Prince. The battle went on. When it was over King Edward congratulated the Prince. He did not give him spurs, i.e. confer knighthood on him (p. 121). The prince had been knighted when the army landed in France. Either Edward used the phrase 'win his spurs' loosely, meaning 'I want the boy to prove his courage,' or else Froissart was inaccurate.

Froissart took a good deal of trouble to get hold of people who could tell him something of value for his chronicle, but it never occurred to him to produce a sketch plan of a battle. The careful, lively artists, who painted queer animals in the margins of books like the Luttrell Psalter, would have produced excellent maps and plans if they had known how. But they did not know how. The Gough map (p. 37) shows how primitive was the cartography of the time. When therefore Froissart's work began to be published, it had gay marginal illustrations, but no maps or plans. These, with a great deal of other information about weapons, uniform and other subjects, which did not interest Froissart, have had to be put together by later historians.

Fighting

The pay of the young Prince of Wales was 20s a day, but he was the only person paid on that scale. The earls who had been worrying about his safety received 6s 8d, barons 4s, knights 2s, archers 3d and Welsh spearmen 2d. These Welsh spearmen were each provided with a tunic and cloak (colour unknown). This was probably the first occasion on which troops fighting for England were clothed by the Government.

The archers wore an iron cap and carried a sword, a dagger and a bow six feet four inches long. The arrows, about a yard long, were of wood with a barbed iron point (a barb makes extraction from the wound more difficult). They were tipped with goose or peacock feathers. Arrows were carried in the belt. The range was about 240 yards and it was possible to fire as many as twelve arrows in a minute. The cross-bow, which Continental armies preferred, had a slower rate of fire.

With the army was a small group of musicians which included five trumpeters, other wind and string instruments and a drummer. (The Scots army, on the other hand, made their own musical noise. Each man carried a horn and all blew together 'to frighten their enemies and cheer themselves'.)

Before the time of Edward III there had been compulsory military service. Edward tried to create a professional army serving for pay and no doubt some villages, especially if they were in any sort of trouble, found the offer of foreign travel, loot and 3d a day attractive. But those who were less willing would find it very difficult to refuse, if the lord of the manor wanted them to go.

The 'men at arms' who consisted of knights and squires, needed less persuading. Although they usually fought on foot in big battles, except when pursuing the enemy, they brought horses and a good deal of portable comfort along with them (including, on one occasion, a pack of hounds—sixty couple). The best horses had to be brought from Spain and were therefore very valuable. Knights usually had four horses with them. The first was always a stallion, the others might be geldings or mares. Numbers one and two were for tournament or mounted fighting. Number three was a pony for travel. Number four carried the luggage.

Squires were usually young men who hoped to become knights but among them were older men who for one reason or another (e.g. expense) had never been knighted. Before a battle they helped a knight to put on his armour, which they had polished. When a knight dismounted ready to fight on foot in a battle, his squire led his charger to the rear.

Sometimes, however, the chargers charged. At Poitiers (1356), for instance, when the English showed signs of losing heart, the Black Prince saved the situation by having the horses brought up, getting his men-at-arms into the saddle and leading them to attack.

Chivalry

'Chivalry' is a word likely to be met with in accounts of the battle of Poitiers. 'King John of France with the flower of his chivalry . . .' 'The chivalry of the Black Prince towards his royal captive . . .'

Originally 'chivalry' meant much the same as 'cavalry'. They both come from a Latin word meaning 'horseman'. Later however 'chivalry' was also used to describe the system of knighthood and the behaviour of knights, when they were behaving well.

To become a knight it was necessary to be of good family, to serve first as a page and then, from about the age of fourteen, as a squire. The age at which squires became knights varied. To be knighted at sixteen, like the Black Prince, was exceptional.

Nowadays knighthoods are usually conferred upon middle-aged men. The ceremony of touching on each shoulder with a sword remains the same but as only a few men are made knights each year the Queen can knight them herself. In the fourteenth century, when everyone of consequence became a knight, the honour could be conferred by others, e.g. by the general after a battle. The famous French knight Bertrand du Guesclin was knighted by his father after a tournament. In spite of the phrase 'to win your spurs' it was not in fact usual to present spurs. They were simply part of the equipment a knight was entitled to wear. They had to be gilded.

Having served as a page and become a squire, Chaucer went campaigning in France (p. 13). He was never knighted, but his lower rank does not seem to have prejudiced him against knights. On the contrary, one of them is given first place among the Canterbury Pilgrims, and it is not generally supposed that Chaucer wrote about him with his tongue in his cheek.

This knight's character was chivalrous. That is to say, he was truthful, honest, polite, modest and brave. To preserve these qualities throughout a lifetime of campaigning in Europe, North Africa and the East was an achievement. The Black Prince did not remain chivalrous until his death. His incurable illness turned him vicious. But at Poitiers his conduct was exemplary to the point of exaggeration. He himself waited on the French King at supper on the evening after the battle and later, when he entered London with his prisoner, it was the prisoner who rode in front, on a fine white horse.

You did not need to be a king in order to be well treated as a prisoner. Standards of knightly behaviour often fell far below those of Chaucer's paragon, but a knight who had surrendered and then promised not to escape generally kept his word. He was thus able to lead quite a tolerable life in his captor's castle until his ransom was paid.

Siege warfare

Castles, like walled towns, still offered a good deal

*The siege
begins*

*Breaching
the wall*

of safety. Gunpowder was just beginning to be used. There is some evidence that three very primitive cannon were used at Crecy, but they can have been of no importance in deciding the battle. Apparatus for attacking fortifications was little different from what the Romans had used. The trebuchet, a kind of giant catapult, flung stones over the walls. Tall wooden towers on wheels helped the besiegers to scale them. Below ground miners dug tunnels. These were not meant to contain explosives. The idea was simply to loosen the foundations of the wall. One method was to insert wooden props smeared with lard as the digging proceeded. These were then set alight and, as they burned through, the masonry above fell in.

The besieged usually had the advantage. It was possible to break the force of the trebuchet missiles by laying out mattresses, hurdles or bundles of hay. If a bell was rung as the engines were seen to be about to fire, there was time for all to take cover. Mines could be detected by hanging up copper basins which were sensitive to vibration. A counter mine could be sunk and sometimes, when the two shafts met, a battle took place underground. Direct assault could be stopped by throwing down bars of red-hot iron, quick-lime and heavy pieces of timber, while the archers fired their arrows or bolts.

Sometimes, however, a determined assault succeeded. When it did, or when a city or castle was starved into surrender, chivalry was apt to be forgotten.

124

Fighting

According to Froissart's account of the siege of Calais (1347) Edward III would have avenged himself on all the citizens, had not Sir Walter Manny persuaded him to accept six leading men, who came to him with ropes round their necks, for his convenience, so that they could be quickly hanged. Only a further intercession by Edward's Queen, Philippa, saved those six citizen's lives. This famous story may not be true, but there is no doubt that the Black Prince, after capturing Limoges in 1367, had its men, women and children massacred.

Fighting for freedom

As we have seen (p. 19) the Black Prince died in 1376 and was buried at Canterbury. The funeral procession passed through Maidstone in Kent. Here there was a prison, whose inmates at this time probably included John Ball.

Ball was a priest who believed in equality and said so. He was therefore frequently locked up. As soon as he was let out he started preaching again, circulating rhyming letters, unsettling the peasants, encouraging them to think that God had meant them to be as good as their masters.

Wat, called Wat Tyler, presumably because he made his living by laying tiles, though he had also served in the army, held similar views.

Five years after the Black Prince's funeral Wat Tyler provided Canterbury with another exciting summer spectacle. The mob of peasants, which he had roused, surged through the streets and burst into the cathedral during Mass. But nobody touched the Black Prince's tomb, nor the mementoes of him which hang above it (Plate I). That would have been the moment for some wag to put on the helmet with its lion crest, for another to seize one of the copper gilt gauntlets or wave the silk embroidered surcoat in the air. But they left these things alone. They were not against the Prince, nor as yet, against 10-year-old King Richard II. They soon marched away towards London, armed with bills and bows (many were ex-soldiers), with a number of unconventional weapons such as knives, cudgels or hatchets, and with a deep sense of injustice.

At Blackheath, Ball preached a sermon on the text:

> *When Adam delved and Eve span*
> *Who was then a gentleman?*

As we have seen (p. 100) he was particularly angry with lawyers, since he felt that they supported the present order of things under which men were unequal. He wanted a new order under which men would be equal. He did not get it. Within a month he had been hanged, drawn and quartered at St Albans. Wat Tyler had already been killed by the Mayor of London. He is one of the few prominent figures in British history commemorated by an opera *(Wat Tyler* by Alan Bush).

Chaucer, in his lodgings over the tower of Aldgate does not seem to have been inconvenienced by these events. John of Gaunt lost his palace, the Savoy, which the mob sacked, burnt and finished off with three barrels of gunpowder which they found in the armoury. Archbishop Sudbury lost his life. Remember Sudbury as a you enter Canterbury from the London road. He built the massive West Gate, through which you pass, and through which only six years after the Peasant's Revolt Chaucer's jolly pilgrims came to the end of their journey (Plate II).

Fighting for Fun

John Ball, Wat Tyler and the rebels fought for freedom—for the right to pay rent for their land instead of being subject to the lord of the manor. Edward III and the Black Prince fought because it was the thing to do and could be profitable. But one form of fighting was conducted principally for entertainment. This was the tournament—organized duelling between knights, usually on horseback.

The ancient Greeks and Romans, though by no means lacking either in toughness or in touchiness, did not resort to single combat as a means of satisfying honour and passing the time. Romans liked bloodshed, but they used gladiators, runaway slaves, Christians or animals. It was probably from among the German tribes that there filtered into Europe the idea that gentlemen might fight each other for fun. Such fights became extremely popular and tournaments were a well established form of upper-class entertainment in

Chaucer's time. Edward III held a number of them at Windsor in connection with his new Order of the Garter (p. 171). Ladies enjoyed the spectacle. The fighters were seldom killed, though sometimes they fought in anger, to settle a quarrel.

The stories of King Arthur and his knights, however fanciful in other respects, contain fairly authentic descriptions of tournaments. Chaucer describes a big one (a hundred knights a side); so does Froissart (at Calais, not long after the incident of the six burghers).

Fighting at sea

Edward III won two naval battles, against the French and the Spaniards off Sluys (1340) and against the Spaniards off Winchelsea (1350). His permanent navy only had about twenty small ships, but in time of war these were supplemented by many others, supplied not only by coastal, but also by inland towns, and by wealthy individuals (e.g. William of Wykeham). In 1373 Lincoln was ordered to supply a ship, fit her out and find a crew 'and to imprison any found contrariant or rebellious in this'. The Cinque Ports (p. 40) had to provide fifty-seven ships for a period of forty days each year.

There was no difference between a warship and a merchant ship except that the former was sometimes fitted with forecastles, aftercastles and fighting-tops (Plate XI). In the battle off Winchelsea the Spaniards at first had the advantage, because their ships were taller.

XI

(Coin)

Gold noble of Edward III showing one of his ships, with rudder. The lilies of France can be seen on his shield. The legend reads:

EDWAR(dus) DEI GRA(tiae) REX ANGL(iae) et FRANC (iae) D(omi) N(us) HYB(erniae) (Edward by the grace of God King of England and France, Lord of Ireland.)

Model of thirteenth century ship, starboard quarter, with steering oar. At the mast head she flies the cross of St. George, in the stern the royal lions and in the bows the flag of the Cinque Ports.

Model of a ship of c1426

Fore-castle and after-castle are now permanent structures and there is a rudder. Since the Kings of England now claimed also to be Kings of France, the lilies of France are with the lions of England on the sail.

XII Windsor Castle

From the Eastern end of Westminster Abbey projects Henry VII's chapel (between two clumps of trees). In Chaucer's time there were houses on this site. He died in one. Nearer the centre, left of Big Ben, is Westminster Hall, the roof of which was built for Richard II

Inset The louvre, originally above a central fire in the hall, smokes again after German bombing in 1941

(The lighter building alongside Westminster Hall is the new House of Commons, rebuilt after bombing.)

They were able to fling stones down on to the English and fire crossbow bolts among them; but the English archers compelled the Spaniards to take cover. Seventeen Spanish ships were boarded and captured during the following night.

The battle was fought, not by sailors, but by soldiers. A naval battle at that time was a land battle fought at sea. Edward III's admirals, one commanding northwards from the Thames, the other southwards and along the channel, were men who had made their names fighting on land. Sir Walter Manny was an admiral for a time.

These naval arrangements sufficed to get our armies safely into France; they also protected England from invasion. This was a real danger, particularly in the year 1386.

A threat of invasion

The French had made tremendous preparations. Fifteen hundred ships were loaded with hay, oats, barley, hard biscuit, wine, salt, meat, onions, flour, casks of eggs, peas, beans, candles, stockings, shoes, spurs, knives, daggers, battle axes, axes to hew with, mattocks, nails, beds, couches, horse-shoes, pots, pans, candlesticks, kitchen utensils, 'and everything', Froissart concludes 'that could be thought necessary to serve man and horse'.

The English garrisoned the ports between Cornwall and the Humber. For instance:

Yarmouth	300 men-at-arms,	600 archers
Dover	500 men-at-arms,	1,200 archers
Sandwich	600 men-at-arms,	1,200 archers
Rye	200 men-at-arms,	600 archers

Watch towers were made by filling wine barrels with sand and piling one on top of another. Beacons were to be lit when the French were sighted.

But the great fleet delayed until it was too late in the year. The operation was postponed. In fact it never took place.

CHAPTER VII

FUN

Books and stories

THE BEST JOKE in the latter half of the fourteenth century did not raise a laugh at the time. It was a hoax, which took in all Europe. A resident of Liège wrote a most plausible account of a journey to Palestine, India and China which in fact he had not made. 'Sir John Mandeville', he called himself and claimed to have been born at St. Albans. The book was extremely readable. Before the end of the century Latin and English translations were available but Chaucer probably read the book before that in the original French. The date of the earliest French manuscript is 1371. Before long the book could be had in German, Danish, Irish and other European languages.

As a rule it is the spectators of a hoax and not the victims, who are amused; but readers of *The Travels of Sir John Mandeville* had nothing to complain of. On the contrary, we now know that they were enjoying a skilled digest of several works of travel and natural history. They could have read the originals, e.g.

131

accounts of the pilgrimage of the German Count Bodensele to Jerusalem (written 1332-8) or of the travels of Friar Odoric in the Far East (written 1330). In theory Chaucer's contemporaries could have read these books just as we nowadays *could* read a number of books which in fact we do not read until they are serialized in a newspaper or summarized in a digest or published in an attractive edition. 'Sir John's' method of spicing travel literature with his imagination and bringing it before a wider public was unorthodox, but gave a great deal of harmless pleasure.

The debt of his contemporaries to 'Sir John Mandeville' was the greater, because light reading-matter was hard to come by. *The Book of the Knight of La Tour Landry,* written in French about the same time as the *Travels* of 'Sir John', became very popular, but it is primarily an account of how girls ought to behave (p. 74); the stories in it are incidental. Here are examples:

1. There was a woman who used to answer her husband in the presence of strangers 'with great villainous words'. This made him ashamed and he asked her not to. But softness did no good. She only grew worse. So 'he smote her with his fist down to earth; and then with his foot he struck her in the visage and brake her nose, and all her life after she had her nose crooked'.

A wife, the story concludes, should not argue with her husband, least of all when other people are present.

132

2. Three merchants riding home from a fair boasted about the obedience of their wives. They agreed that whichever of them should prove to have the most disobedient wife should stand the other two a dinner. The test was to be an order to leap into a basin without any previous warning, other than the words, 'Look, wife, that whatsoever I command be done'.

In the first merchant's house, when the basin had been put on the floor and his wife had been ordered to jump into it, she asked 'Why?'

'Because it is my wish,' answered the merchant.

'Tell me *why*,' said the wife and firmly refused to do as she was told.

'So her husband up with his fist, and gave her two or three great strokes; and then they went to the second merchant's house.'

The second wife reacted like the first, so her husband took a stick and beat her.

The third wife on the other hand so loved and feared her husband that when, as she thought, he told her to jump on the table she did so, broke the glasses and scattered the food over the floor. In fact the knight had only asked for salt to be put on the table (since eggs had been served) but his wife mistook the French 'sel' (salt) for 'seyle' which in old French meant 'jump'. Everyone thought this very funny. 'There was much mirth and laughing.' The other two merchants said this wife had proved herself quite obedient enough without being asked to jump into a basin and they agreed that they

133

had lost their bet. The wife was greatly praised for her
obedience and was not beaten as the other two had been.

The Ménagier of Paris (p. 73) contains a whole series
of similar stories, emphasizing that a wife should stoop
to any folly without question if her husband orders
her. Instead of jumping into basins the wives in these
stories are asked for instance to count up to four or to
jump over a stick. But the moral is the same.

Mandeville's *Travels, The Book of the Knight of La
Tour Landry* and *The Ménagier of Paris,* were all written first in French. How did you manage if you only
knew English?

The chances were that if you only knew English, you
did not rely very much on books for entertainment or
instruction. It is true that French, after being the language of the ruling classes since the time of William the
Conqueror, was now giving place to English. To cele-
brate his fiftieth birthday (1362) Edward III had agreed
to make English the official language of the Lawcourts.
But as yet very little English prose had been written,
and this was not easily obtainable. *The Ladder of Per-
fection,* by Walter Hilton was only intended for mystics.
Wycliffe's translation of the Bible circulated mainly
amongst his followers. The only other major prose
works in English were also translations—Mandeville's
Travels, put into English by an unknown hand (before
his exposure 'Sir John' was thought to have written the
French and English versions himself and was hailed as

134

the 'Father of English prose') and two translations by
John Trevisa, a Cornishman who obtained a fellow-
ship at the Queen's College, Oxford, while Wycliffe was
there, and later became chaplain to Lord Berkeley in
Gloucestershire.

The works which Trevisa translated (both from the
Latin) were encyclopedias of a sort. Trevisa plunged
doggedly ahead, inserting his own comments here and
there and not ashamed, when floored, to write 'God
knows what this means'. He is the earliest author to be
quoted in the Oxford Book of English Prose, but no
'Father of English Prose' can be said to be generally
recognized, in the way that Chaucer is generally recognized as the Father of English Poetry.

It is clear that, despite Trevisa's industry, a man or
woman who liked reading prose would have been badly
off in Chaucer's lifetime, had English been the only
language he or she knew. Anyone interested in books
would almost certainly have known Latin and French,
and would have done most of his reading in those
languages. (Chaucer knew Italian as well.)

For poetry of course, an Englishman was not depen-
dent on translations; but, since all books had to be
copied by hand, new work (e.g. by Chaucer, Langland
or Gower) did not quickly reach a wide public.

A further obstacle in the way of those who might
have enjoyed reading was the high price of books. To
own a book then may be compared to owning an
original painting nowadays—the vast majority of

people would not have dreamt of it. Even the smallest library was beyond the reach of most poor scholars. Students today sometimes protest that they cannot afford to buy books, but it has been estimated that, if Chaucer's 'Clerk of Oxenford' really had twenty volumes of Aristotle at the head of his bed (as stated in the *Prologue*), they must have cost him as much as three town houses.

In 1331, Edward III bought a book which cost him £66 13s 4d. An idea of the value of this sum can be gained from the fact that not long before £7 10s bought ten oxen, £4 twenty pigs and £6 twenty-four swans. Carpenters, you may remember, earned 3d a day at that time and a book of Latin extracts for a schoolboy was thought good value at 12s (p. 69).

In view of the high cost of books, one might have expected them to be treated with great care. Some were —the Luttrell Psalter and Queen Mary's Psalter, to give two famous examples which can still be seen in the British Museum. Humbler books fared worse, according to the following outburst by the Bishop of Exeter, (p. 85) writing when Chaucer was five, a year before Crecy. Scholars, he complains, use their long, dirty, black finger-nails to mark their favourite passages (there were no pencils). They use straws as book-marks. They eat fruit or cheese over a book or rest a cup on it. They fall asleep over it and crease the pages. They ornament the margins or write in them. Worse still, they cut off the margins to use for writing

136

letters. (Books were written on parchment. Paper however was known, though probably not yet manufactured in England.)

Fortunately, reading to oneself is not the only way of enjoying a story. Chaucer's poems were sometimes read aloud or recited, by the poet himself. His audiences, however, were distinguished people. Ordinary men and women found that priests and friars told some of the best stories. A selection of their repertory was collected together during the fourteenth century into a book called *Gesta Romanorum,* so we have some idea of what kind of story people expected in the course of a sermon. *Gesta Romanorum* means 'Deeds of the Romans' but does not properly describe the collection, which in fact contains stories from all kinds of sources. Here is an example, put shortly.

Two knights (call them A and B) rode away together. A returned without B so he was accused of having murdered B and condemned to death by the king. Another knight, C, was ordered to carry out the sentence.

As C was leading A to the place of execution they met B, who, far from having been murdered, looked fit and well.

So they all lived happily ever after? Oh, no. The king was furious that his sentence had not been carried out. He instantly condemned all three to death for the following reasons:

A, because he had already been condemned (for murdering B);

137

B, because his disappearance had caused A to be condemned and he was therefore guilty of A's death;

C, because he had been ordered to execute A and had not done so.

What is the moral? Chaucer makes a friar tell this story in the course of the Summoner's Tale, simply as an example of the lengths a man (in this case the king) will go to if he does not try to curb his ill-temper. On the other hand in the *Gesta Romanorum* the story is headed 'Of Equity' and it begins with the statement that the king was 'remarkable for his inflexible justice'.

Miracle Plays

Ideas of what makes a good story have changed since the fourteenth century, but on the level of farce we are closer to Chaucer's time. Surprisingly, it is the miracle plays, based on Bible stories, which make this clear. For example, Noah is represented in one of these plays as a hen-pecked husband. From the moment that the ark begins to take shape Noah's wife makes it quite clear that she is not going to co-operate. (She is very different from the model wives mentioned above, who jump on to tables or over sticks at the bidding of their husbands).

> Noah: *Good wife, do now as I thee bid.*
> Noah's wife: *By Christ, not ere I see more need,*
> *Though thou stand all the day and stare.*

When the ark is built Noah's wife still refuses to leave her friends.

'Come in wife, in the devil's name!' shouts Noah.

'Shall we all fetch her in?' asks Ham. Aided by Japheth and Shem he bundles his mother on board. 'Welcome!' says Noah. 'Take that!' says she. The stage direction, 'She boxes him on the ear' is the last we hear of her. The long speeches by Noah and God which conclude the play must have seemed an anti-climax to many members of the audience.

Noah's Flood with other medieval miracle plays based on the Old and New Testament, is published in the 'Everyman' edition. I have seen it performed successfully by schoolchildren, with one of the teachers reading the part of God behind the scenes.

In the original play God would have been impersonated on the stage like the other characters. The 'stage' was sometimes a cart with platforms on two levels. The lower was curtained and served as a dressing-room. The higher was the stage. The carts, which were equipped and manned by companies from different trades (the story of Noah's ark was, appropriately, assigned to the shipwrights) were wheeled round the town and halted at certain points where the plays were presented. There could be as many as twenty-four carts. Anyone who wanted to see all the plays had only to take up a position at one of these points, wait and hope that it would not rain. Citizens thus had entertainment brought to their homes in a way that did not happen again until the arrival of television.

Television, however, is with us daily. Miracle plays usually took place at the feast of Corpus Christi. This

139

was a new Christian feast introduced in 1311. It falls on the Thursday after Trinity Sunday and is therefore at a time of year when there is at least a chance of the weather being kind to open-air play-acting.

Among the most famous plays were those at Chester, Coventry and York (where a modernized version has been given in recent years); but many other towns had plays and Corpus Christi was not the only day when they were performed.

Although the actors were amateurs, who normally earned their living as craftsmen, they were paid for their performance. At Hull Noah was paid 1s; God and Noah's wife got less. At Coventry one man had the two duties of hanging Judas and crowing like a cock. He got 4d for each—8d in all.

For the music professional assistance was needed and minstrels were engaged. Costumes and properties were simple. As can be seen from painting and sculpture of the time audiences expected Biblical characters to be dressed like fourteenth-century Englishmen. Angels, however, were provided with wings and in the play about the Last Judgment saved souls were clothed in white to distinguish them from the damned, who were in black. Somehow, in spite of the small space available, real fire was kindled in the mouth of the stage hell, while thunders rumbled.

Wycliffe and his followers strongly disapproved of all this.

Minstrels

Minstrels, dancers and acrobats travelled the country and performed in the halls of castles or in the market place. There were all kinds of minstrels. You might say that they ranged from the level of a sea-side concert-party to that of international opera. But even that parallel does not do justice to the most famous minstrels.

An acrobat entertains at dinner

These were poets and musicians who counted kings among their friends. It was they who developed the great romances such as the *Song of Roland* and *King Arthur*. But by the second half of the fourteenth century the great days of the minstrels were over. Most of them were by now simply entertainers—usually noisy and vulgar. People of good taste who, two hundred years before, might themselves have competed with

141

minstrels in the making of poetry and song now had books or recitations by Chaucer to turn to.

Not that such recitations were so very far removed

A minstrel playing the bagpipes

from the kind of entertainment that the better minstrels had given. Chaucer often chose subjects from the Romances (e.g. *Troilus and Criseyde*) and there is a possibility that he meant this poem to be sung rather

142

than recited. Was Chaucer a minstrel? The word is not used to describe him, partly because of the more intimate atmosphere in which he worked—the garden or the solar, rather than the crowded hall. But he was in the minstrel tradition.

Music

The fact that the great age of minstrels was over and that the golden age of English music under Elizabeth I was still far ahead, does not mean that Chaucer's England lay in a state of toneless insulation, broken only by bird song and abbey choirs. Plenty of informal music was made. The Squire in the *Prologue* sang and played the flute; the Friar sang and played the hurdy-gurdy (a sort of barrel organ or musical box); the Miller played the bagpipes. Nor was the singing only in unison. The Pardoner and the Summoner sang a duet ('Come hither love to me'). 'Sumer is icumen in', a song in six parts which is still popular, was already at least a hundred years old.

Carols

The miracle plays which by Chaucer's time were performed in the streets, as described earlier in this chapter, developed from simple scenes performed in church. This was not the only fun connected with church-going. There were the wall paintings, the stained glass, the stories from the pulpit; and, occasionally, there was carolling. To 'carol' meant originally to 'dance in a ring'. Dancing in church was one of the customs taken over by Christianity from the pagan religions which it superseded. At Christmas it was usual to dance round the crib (introduced by St Francis). The dancers sang and in time the word 'carol' was used to describe simple, gay songs, instead of the dance which accompanied them.

In the *Oxford Book of Carols* (which contains carols for all seasons, not only for Christmas) there is one, 'Now welcome, Summer, with thy sunne soft', whose author is given as Geoffrey Chaucer, but this carol in fact consists of words taken from one of Chaucer's long poems and set to a traditional Irish tune. Chaucer did not write it as a carol. Among the carols sung in King's College Chapel, Cambridge, at Christmas 1957, only one, 'In dulci jubilo' is described as 'Fourteenth Century' and it is a translation from German, with about half its lines in Latin. The words of 'Adam lay ybounden' may have been known in the fourteenth century, though our earliest MS. of them is later; but the tune to which it was sung in King's College Chapel was modern.

The truth is that hardly anything is known of carols in Chaucer's time. The earliest collection of carols that survives is from the fifteenth century.

The Boy Bishop

People seldom dance in churches now. Seville Cathedral is an exception. There at certain festivals the choir-

144

boys dance with castanets and sing in front of the high-altar. Even there, however, they do not elect a Boy Bishop. That was another Christian custom with non-Christian origins. It seems now to have fallen into disuse completely.

For a brief period during the Roman winter festival, the 'Saturnalia', slaves ruled, while masters and mistresses obeyed. Boy Bishops were a survival of this idea. The most suitable chorister was chosen. He walked in procession on Holy Innocents' Day (December 28th) and sometimes preached a sermon, which had been written for him.

So far, you may think his position not worth competing for; but it offered opportunities for getting one's own back on the clergy. The mock authority of the boys varied from place to place, but we know that they enjoyed assigning a very humble part in the procession to high church dignitaries, because the high Church dignitaries made regulations, which survive, saying that this was going too far.

Boy Bishops and their chorister attendants also had good opportunities for over-eating and making money. At York in 1396 veal, mutton, sausages, duck, chicken, ale and wine were on the menu. After Innocents' Day the Bishop and six attendants paid visits on horse-back throughout the diocese (e.g. to Leeds, Bridlington and Beverley). A collection was taken on the way which more than covered expenses.

Winchester College had a Boy Bishop every year. He

K

wore a mitre made of a piece of cloth of gold given by
William of Wykeham and carried a copper gilt crosier.
On one occasion he could afford to give 1s 8d to dancers
who entertained him.

Games

If you write a play about Chaucer, you should not
introduce a scene in which he is shown sitting down to
a game of cards. He never mentions the game in his

*Gambling with dice. The man on the right has staked
his clothes and lost all*

poems. It seems only to have reached England from the
Continent towards the end of the fourteenth century.

'Tables', chess, dice and draughts were the popular
adult indoor games of Chaucer's time, among those—
a minority—who had leisure, elbow-room, fuel and
light. The clergy, however, were not allowed to play.

'Tables' or backgammon is the ancestor of the hundreds of games in which dice are thrown and players
move their counters forward, or wait a turn or are sent
back to an earlier point on the board.

Chess nowadays has come to be considered a game

that only clever people can play. This was not so in the fourteenth century. Edward III played, knights played, ladies played. Lovers could converse conveniently over the chessboard. Bets were laid on the results of chess matches and fights sometimes broke out when one of the players proved to be a bad loser. Minstrels carried chessmen and could offer their patrons a game.

Chess had reached Europe from the East some cen-

A king playing chess

turies earlier. The pieces were often large and exquisitely carved. The game was similar to modern chess but the moves and the names of the pieces were not yet uniform throughout Europe. The queen was also known as the 'Firz' from the Persian 'Vizier'. (No female piece was allowed on the Persian chessboard. The East was even more of a man's world than the West, which is saying something.) The Queen had not yet attained the wide power which she has now. She could only move one square diagonally. 'Castling' had not yet been introduced, but the king could leap two or sometimes three squares. Pawns could not yet make a

147

first move of two squares. But 'problems'—artificial positions from which the solver must mate in a certain number of moves—had already reached Europe from the East.

Dances, judging from the few pictures we have, were simple, like the carolling in church mentioned earlier in this chapter. Groups of men and women revolved in circles. There was no dancing in couples, still less cheek

A dance

to cheek, although kissing as a form of greeting between men and women was much commoner in those days than it is now (p. 102).

A number of indoor games which would now be thought childish were played, such as blindman's buff, or hot-cockles, in which a player, kneeling and blindfolded, with his hand held out behind, had to guess who had slapped it.

Pets

We have met the Prioress's illicit little dogs (p. 93). Ladies also kept birds, particularly magpies, because they could be taught to speak (parrots were still rare in this country). There is no reason to suppose that a magpie could acquire a wider vocabulary then than now, but stories credited them with more or less human powers. One of the stories in *The Book of the Knight of La Tour Landry* introduces a magpie, who spies on his master's wife and reports her for having caught and

A cage of birds

eaten a large eel, which the master was keeping in his pond ready for some great feast.

Some monkeys were kept, but cats were not popular. They were associated in people's minds with witches. Nuns were allowed to keep cats but seem to have preferred the forbidden dogs.

Out of doors

Hawking or falconry, hunting the stag and shooting game were all sports in which women as well as men

149

could join if they were wealthy. Wrestling, later enjoyed by Henry VIII, was not yet an upper-class pastime. Among the poorer classes target practice with the bow was insisted on by law. From the wording of such laws

Ladies hawking

(e.g. 1363, 1388) we know that people preferred to play ball or coits 'and other such inopportune games'. John of Gaunt increased the number of tempting alternatives by introducing the Morris dance from Spain.

Playing ball

A whipping-top

Ladies rode astride as well as side-saddle during this period. Richard II's wife Anne of Bohemia was formerly thought to have introduced the side-saddle into England, but it is now believed to have reached this country during the twelfth century.

Ladies hunting the stag; the one on horseback rides astride

Pilgrimages

Nobody can read the *Prologue* without forming the opinion that, although pious people still took part, many pilgrims were simply out for a good holiday. The

151

journey to the shrines of St Thomas of Canterbury or Our Lady of Walsingham (Norfolk) could never be acutely arduous and might well be very good fun. On the other hand to undertake a voyage to the shrine of St James of Compostella in Spain sometimes needed powers of endurance which only real piety could have sustained. The preliminary irritants are familiar to us still. A passport had to be obtained and there were currency restrictions. Pilgrims had to swear not to take out of England more gold or silver than they needed for the journey. Furthermore, they were forbidden to reveal the secrets of the kingdom.

After all this they were crowded on board some little ship at Southampton or Dartmouth or Saltash. Sixty to a hundred was the usual number carried. Everyone was sick except the crew, who pushed the pilgrims about, accused them of hindering the working of the ship, and made a great show of eating and drinking beer.

There were shrines all over Europe. Not all the relics they displayed were genuine. There was one head of John the Baptist at Amiens and another at Constantinople.

Finally, in case any reader should think that pilgrimages are a thing of the past, it should be remembered that Lourdes now attracts thousands more worshippers every year than ever took the road to Canterbury.

CHAPTER VIII

IN TROUBLE

IN LONDON ONE midnight six young men filled a barrel with stones and sent it rolling through Gracechurch Street to London Bridge 'to the great terror of the neighbours'. This was too much for the watchman of the Ward to deal with. He 'raised the hue and cry', i.e. he shouted for help. His cries were answered. The young men were arrested and put in a prison called the Tun.

Minor offences committed in London were tried in the Mayor's Court. There the six young men duly appeared. A jury had been summoned. The jury in those days consisted of a group of witnesses. They swore in turn that the offence had been committed. The young men were found guilty. Unfortunately we do not know how they were punished.

Thomas atte Chirche

In the above case citizens did their duty when the hue and cry was raised and an arrest followed. The case of Thomas atte Chirche was much less satisfactory, except from the point of view of Thomas atte Chirche.

Late in the afternoon of an October day Thomas, squire to the Earl of Arundel, was riding with another man along Thames Street, towards the Tower, when he ran his horse against a woman with a baby and nearly knocked her over. A man called John saw this and shouted to the two men that they should ride more carefully, whereupon Thomas drew his sword and ran it into John's right side. The wound was later described as two inches long and five inches deep. John was just able to walk home to the room which he rented in a house not far away; he died there next day. But, although there were plenty of people in the street at the time, no one laid hold of Thomas or his companion. They both rode on and escaped.

It is possible that we only have half of this story. There may have been an arrest later. Although there was rivalry between towns, there was also co-operation. Officials exchanged letters about criminals and suspects. In the present case, however, it seems all too probable that Thomas atte Chirche escaped punishment. He was a squire of the Earl of Arundel and great men were accustomed to influence the course of justice by a show of force. Once Thomas had escaped from London he could count on a gang of armed Arundel retainers clamouring outside any court where he was brought to trial.

The indifference of the onlookers, who saw the

assault, but let Thomas get away, is not peculiar to Chaucer's time. The responsibility of the public to help in arresting a criminal has not changed in the last six hundred years, nor has the tendency of many people to shirk it. It is possible at the present day for a man to be struggling with a burglar in a crowded street without anyone coming to his help.

The robber knights

If a man could get away with manslaughter in a crowded London street, it is not surprising that law was difficult to enforce in the open country, particularly when the criminals were influential people. In the following case all of them were knights.

One Friday in 1342 two servants left Lichfield with two horses which were loaded with silk and groceries worth £40. They were on their way to Stafford market. Near Cannock Wood a knight, Sir Robert de Rideware, and two of his squires were lying in wait. They fell upon the two men. One escaped, but the other, with the merchandise, was taken to a near-by priory where other knights were waiting. Here the spoil was divided. The whole party then rode to a convent and asked for hospitality. Sir Robert said they were retainers of the King, exhausted after a long day's riding on official business. But the Abbess was not deceived and refused to admit the party, who then robbed her barns and slept in them.

Meanwhile the escaped servant, after following the

party to the convent, had managed to summon the sheriff, an officer who carried on his shoulders many of the responsibilities of a modern county constabulary. The sheriff and a party of volunteers rode to the convent. After a stiff fight the knights fled, leaving the booty and four of their company behind. Those four were beheaded on the spot. But Sir Robert was not one of them. He persuaded a relative to join him, the combined force then attacked the sheriff and recaptured the merchandise.

The sheriff's ardour seems now to have cooled. He could do nothing more for the merchants who had been robbed; and when they went to Stafford, presumably hoping to bring the matter before the visiting royal judges, they were attacked by Sir Robert's men at the gates. All they could do was go back to Lichfield.

After this sad story it is a relief to return to some cases in London where justice seems to have been done.

Bad food

A customer asked the proprietor of a cook-shop for a reduction in price 'because I have bought no flesh but at your shop for the last seven years'. 'What!' was the reply, 'For so long a time, and you are still alive!' There is a suggestion here that regulations about fair trading were taken about as seriously in Chaucer's time as parking regulations are taken by some motorists today. Nevertheless cases of prosecution for selling impure food and giving short weight appear more frequently in fourteenth-century records than they do in the weekly local newspaper today.

On May 8th, 1382 in the afternoon, five citizens of Somerset came before the Mayor and aldermen with two pieces of cooked fish, 'rotten and stinking and unwholesome for man', which they had bought at a cookshop in Bread Street at noon. The cook had assured them that the fish was good.

You can see those five citizens of Somerset. They were up in London on business. It was a hot summer day. The cook-shop fish was past its prime. Any of the regular customers might have eaten it without bothering, but the Somerset men were accustomed to fresh fish. Besides, being strangers in the city, they had time on their hands. They made a formal complaint.

The Mayor sent for the cook, who admitted selling the fish, but still insisted that it was good and wholesome. It is surprising to us that the condition of the fish could admit of any argument; however, nostrils were probably less sensitive then. Anyhow, the Mayor summoned a jury—twelve reputable men, neighbours of the cook. Each of them had a sniff at the fish. Their verdict was unanimous. The fish was 'rotten, stinking and unwholesome for man'.

The cook was ordered to repay the price of the fish (sixpence), to stand in the pillory for an hour and to have the fish burned beneath him (so that both he and the public would remember why he was there).

Making the punishment fit the crime in this way was not unusual. For instance: John Penrose, convicted of selling bad wine, was forced to drink some of it and have the remainder poured over his head. Robert Porter, convicted of inserting a piece of iron in a penny loaf of bread (to make it weigh more), was put in the pillory for an hour with the loaf and the piece of iron hung round his neck. Alice de Caustone sold ale from a measure which was supposed to be a quart, but in fact had an inch and a half of pitch in the bottom; she was put in the pillory and half of her false measure was hung beside her. (Presumably it was cut vertically, so as to show the false bottom.) Richard Scot invited two visiting Scots from Dumfries into his house and by using false dice won 40s and a knife (value 4s) off them. He had to pay back 44s and a further 1s 8d and had to stand in the pillory for an hour with the dice round his neck. After that he was put in Newgate prison and was taken back to the pillory on the two following days 'with trumpets and pipes'. Punishment with music was common. It drew attention to the culprit, and increased the embarrassment of his position, while giving additional pleasure to the onlookers.

The Manor Court

Many of the offences committed outside the towns consisted in failure to perform whatever services were owed to the Lord of the Manor, and they were dealt with in the Manor Court, held every six weeks. Here

Chaucer's Reeve would have appeared with a list of transgressors whom he wanted to be punished. X had put too many beasts on the common. Y had failed to repair his house. Z had flooded the highway by neglecting to clean out a ditch. A had taken timber from the lord's wood without leave. B had come late to work. C had been insolent. A fine of 1d or 2d was the usual penalty. There were also disputes between tenants to be settled—one man's beasts had trespassed on another's wheat, or an agreement for mutual help over ploughing had been broken.

But some of the heaviest penalties exacted at the Manor Court were not fines for committing offences. They were traditional payments due from a tenant to his lord. If he wanted permission for his daughter to marry, he had to pay; if a son showed promise and he wanted permission to send him away for schooling, in the hope of his becoming a priest, the permission had to be paid for; if a holding fell vacant, whoever took it over paid a fine on entry; finally, when a tenant died, his family were liable for 'heriot'—the surrender of the dead man's best beast.

There had been a time when every important landowner, whether abbot or baron, had his own gallows. But that time was now passed. Murder and theft of goods valued at more than 1s, crimes for which hanging was the penalty, were dealt with by a Justice of the Peace (then, as now, an amateur) or by the King's judges (professionals—like Chaucer's Man of Law).

who held assizes in certain towns four times a year. Of course the Justice of the Peace who tried a man for murder might also happen to be his feudal lord; but the lord or one of his officials, exacted fines in the Manor Court as a master, whereas, sitting as a J.P., he was the King's servant. To the man with the noose round his neck it mattered little whether he was about

The gallows, the wheel (a form of torture), and the hurdle on which criminals were dragged to execution

to swing for his King or his lord. Detached observers however agree that royal justice was the better.

Not only had the lord of the manor lost his gallows. He had also, by the time Chaucer was born, lost some of his serfs. Many of these losses were incurred by agreement, when a lord needed money more than services. A request was made in the Manor Court and an appropriate payment was made. But payments, however appropriate from the lord's point of view, were not to everybody's taste and the Manor Court regularly listened to reports of serfs who had simply run away.

What could the Court do about these fugitives? Not

very much. If they were brought back within four days they could be fined and set to work again; after four days they had to await trial by the King's judges. If they remained at liberty for a year and a day they were usually considered free.

On the run

Escaping from his lord's men was not the runaway serf's only problem. He had to find work. This was not always easy. Towns were good places of refuge but members of the various trades were jealous of competition. A fugitive who had done skilled work on his lord's estate—carpentry, for instance—could not expect to set up immediately as a carpenter in, say, Bristol or Norwich; but it was possible for a fugitive to get work as a day labourer on a manor far from his own. Plenty of lords needed paid workers to supplement the services done by their serfs. Such work, however, took some finding and might not last for long. When therefore the Black Death in 1349 killed between half and a third of the population, it became much easier to find work. Employers, whether in town or country, were desperate for work-people. Not only could a workman have his pick of jobs; he could also get higher wages. A golden age was at hand. Or so it seemed.

'F' for 'Falsity'

In fact the age which was at hand was one of increasing bitterness, culminating in the Revolt of 1381. The need for labour made landowners much less willing to allow serfs to exchange services for a money rent, while the free labourers had their freedom curtailed once more by the Statute of Labourers (1351) and later en-actments. Wages were fixed at the 1346 rate and the movements of all country labourers were restricted, so that they could not move from one employer to some other, who they thought would treat them better.

The stocks—a sedentary form of the pillory—now appear. They are a form of punishment of which little is heard during Norman and Plantagenet times, but every

The stocks

village was now ordered to erect them. There is no evidence that every village immediately did so, but they gradually became an established form of punishment and some stocks remained in use until a century ago.

Another penalty which justices were encouraged to use was branding with an 'F' on the forehead ('F' for the 'falsity' of the man who tried to better himself by moving).

In Trouble

Wages rose nevertheless and labourers became more prosperous; but the result of more food combined with less liberty was that muscle and resentment grew simultaneously, until the chance came for both to have free rein for a few days in the summer of 1381.

Church courts

You may remember that William of Wykeham made regulations against rowdyism in the chapel of Winchester College and that the behaviour both of clergy and congregation in churches and cathedrals was often bad. A further example is to be found in the following report of behaviour at St Paul's during the autumn of 1385. Salesmen were to be found inside the cathedral, offering all sorts of merchandise, almost every day, especially on feast days; outside, a gang of boys made a habit of throwing stones and shooting arrows at the rooks, pigeons and other birds which nested in the walls and perches of the cathedral. This gang also played ball inside the cathedral, breaking windows and damaging statues.

Nowadays damage to a church would be dealt with by the police in the same way as damage to any other sort of property; but in Chaucer's time the church had its own courts with powers to punish certain offences. In the case quoted above the Bishop of London threatened the malefactors with excommunication. We are not told that it was necessary to bring them to trial, but no one would be sorry to hear that they had

163

been. On the other hand the type of immorality with which the church courts mainly dealt consisted not of rowdyism, but of improper love-making.

There was nothing either bad or extraordinary in having immorality punished in a court of law. Some immorality still is. The trouble was that the church courts and their officials were so often ready to settle for a cash payment. For instance Chaucer's Summoner, as we have seen (p. 93), used to try and catch people kissing; his motive, however, was not to prevent A's husband kissing B's wife and thus wrecking the happiness of two families. All he was interested in was frightening the two people concerned into bribing him not to summon them before the Archdeacon's court. And if they had been taken to court all the Archdeacon would have been interested in was the size of fine he could get them to pay. 'Don't worry about being cursed by the Archdeacon,' said the Summoner in effect, 'it's not your soul but your purse he's interested in.'

Heresy, however, was another matter. Heresy—disagreement with the teachings of the Church—was hardly known in England in the three centuries before Wycliffe began his preaching. There had been Protestant movements in Italy and France and the Inquisition was already at work there. But in England it had not yet been found necessary to correct opinions by torture and burning at the stake.

When the Lollards began to appear in towns and villages and were often welcomed by influential people,

164

the Summoners were faced with a new situation. Lollards did not yield to blackmail. But they did yield to the threats of Bishops during the early days of the movement. There was the case of William Smith, a Lollard who chopped up an image of St Catherine for firewood, as a gesture against superstition. His case was not one of the routine offences which were delegated to the Archdeacon. It was the Bishop himself who thundered at Smith. The majestic robes, the cross held threateningly aloft against a background of candles, the jangling bells and the awe-inspiring voice of authority had their effect. Smith agreed to a penance, part of which was to walk with an image of St Catherine in his hand.

At Lincoln, as early as 1382, a Lollard was condemned to the stake, but John of Gaunt interceded for him. The Lollard recanted and was set free. It was only after Chaucer's death, that the law toughened (e.g. the law 'On the burning of heretics', 1401). The Lollards toughened too. But that story belongs to the fifteenth century.

Loopholes

Thomas atte Chirche and Sir Robert de Rideware (p. 153-6) are two examples of men who committed crimes and paid no penalty. The policing both of town and country was rudimentary. In view of this it is surprising to find two officially recognized loopholes in the system of justice to which Chaucer and his contemporaries were subject. Both these loopholes were provided by the Church. They were—Sanctuary, and Benefit of Clergy.

Sanctuary

Nowadays a sanctuary is a safe place for birds. In Chaucer's time Sanctuary was a safe place for criminals and debtors. They could take refuge in any church. Once they were inside the precincts the King's officers might not touch them. The officers could of course wait outside, but the man they were after had two ways of eluding them. Either he could slip through the guards at night, or he could come to the door of the church, confess himself guilty and 'abjure the realm'. This meant that he was under oath to proceed to the coast, bare-headed, bare-foot and carrying a wooden cross, by the most direct route. Once there he had to leave the kingdom by the next ship. Since the oath of most 'Sanctuary men' was not worth very much, this journey to the coast, even when it was made under escort, provided further opportunities for escape (but sometimes it provided an opportunity for outraged citizens to pursue the malefactor and lynch him).

Thus Sanctuary, while at first sight appearing to be a merciful institution, in fact only increased the difficulty of preserving law and order. It is not surprising that pursuers were sometimes willing to take the risk of going into a church and dragging out the man they wanted. This however was a risky procedure. A man called Nicholas Poster who helped to drag some criminals from a church was sentenced by the Bishop of Durham to be whipped in front of the church door, bare-headed, bare-foot and in his shirt, on Monday, Tuesday and Wednesday of Whit-week. On each occasion he had to proclaim the reason for his penance. He was then taken to the door of the cathedral and the process was repeated. This, remember, was the penalty not for committing theft or murder, but for being over-zealous in arresting those who had.

In the Poet's Corner of Westminster Abbey, not far from Chaucer's tomb, you can see the grave of a knight named Hawle. He was one of the more reputable Sanctuary men. He reached Westminster Abbey after escaping from the Tower, where he had been confined for what now seem to be insufficient reasons. But the Governor of the Tower was determined to get him back. His men found Hawle singing Mass with the monks. They tried to arrest him; he drew his sword, beat them back and ran. The Governor's men had to chase him twice round the choir before they caught and killed him.

Archbishop Sudbury excommunicated the Governor of the Tower and all those who had helped him. King Richard supported the Governor. The atmosphere at Westminster was so strained that Parliament met at Gloucester. The whole question of Sanctuary was discussed. It was clear that this ancient custom not only gave shelter to criminals and debtors who did not deserve it, but it also led to scandalous incidents in church, such as the murder of Hawle.

The modern method of dealing with such a complicated and controversial subject is to appoint a Royal Commission. Richard's Parliament summoned learned men to argue the matter in their presence. Wycliffe was one of these. He was against Sanctuary. However, as sometimes happens now after a Royal Commission has reported, hardly anything was done. The right of Sanctuary and its attendant evils remained.

Benefit of Clergy

In spite of the difficulties of catching thieves and murderers, some of them were caught and hanged. It was noticeable however that a tonsured head seldom found its way into a noose. This was not because there were no tonsured rogues but because clerics were allowed to be tried in church courts, which treated them leniently. This was another loophole in the law which was not stopped until long after Chaucer's time.

CHAPTER IX

THE COURT

CHESS KINGS, YOU may remember, had not yet learnt to castle in the fourteenth century (p. 147). Real kings however castled a great deal. In the year 1299 Edward I moved seventy-five times from one castle or religious house to another (i.e. an average of three times a fortnight). Frequent moves were essential, since a long stay in one place crippled the neighbourhood. Officers called 'purveyors' went ahead of the royal party and requisitioned corn, hay, oats, beer, meat and the carts necessary to transport these provisions. Payment was promised but was often not made. Racketeers who were not purveyors pretended that they were. Edward III knew about all this and tried, without success, to stop it. In view of the present-day tendency to try to keep people happy by giving them fancy names (e.g. road sweepers have become 'road orderlies', dustmen are 'refuse collectors', anyone with a smattering of mechanical know-how is a 'technologist') it is interesting to note that Edward tried to make his purveyors better loved by formally altering their designation to 'buyers'.

A palace garden with a king and queen playing chess

Towns were not exempt from royal visits. As the King and his numerous escort approached, an officer went ahead to arrange accommodation. He noted the best-looking houses and had them marked with chalk. The inmates were then informed that they must be hosts to certain members of the court.

Sometimes war with Scotland was the reason for the

King's movements. Edward III could not come south to meet Philippa when she arrived from Hainault for the first time. She had to make the journey north. They were married on January 24th, 1328, at York, where they stayed till Easter. When peace with Scotland was made they moved by way of Lincoln and Northampton to a summer palace at Woodstock, near Oxford. There was another palace at Eltham, south of London, but Woodstock was at this time Queen Philippa's favourite. There, in June 1330, the Black Prince was born. But when war against Scotland started again, the Queen followed her husband north, where she was besieged in Bamborough Castle. She was often in the north and on the Continent, but she also found time to pay visits to the colony of Flemish weavers, her compatriots, which was forming at Norwich, as a result of Edward's plan to make England a producer of fine cloth as well as a producer of fine wool.

Edward III and Windsor Castle

Edward III had been born at Windsor and he liked the place. He chose it as the headquarters of the Order of the Garter which he founded in 1348. The patron of the Order was St George and it was supposed to be a revival of King Arthur's Round Table. The motto chosen was 'Honi soit qui mal y pense'.

St George had been specially honoured in England since before the Norman conquest. Stories of King

171

Arthur and his knights were universally popular. The garter and the motto are less easily explained. Froissart fails us here. It is not till the reign of Henry VII that the now popular account of what happened first appeared. According to this story a lady dropped her garter while dancing with the King (it is remarkable that garters did not come undone more often in those pre-elastic days). Edward picked the garter up. Some members of the court smirked. Edward, annoyed, said 'Honi soit qui mal y pense' ('Evil to him who evil thinks').

The purpose of the foundation with its attendant tournaments and banquets was to bring fighters of renown to Edward's court, thereby increasing his military strength and his European reputation. The Order contained twenty-five knights (in addition to the King) a college of priests and twenty-six knights who had become impoverished owing to having had to ransom themselves in the French wars. These 'poor' knights were to live at Windsor and pray for the, normally, non-resident knights of the Garter. The extensive building works which Edward embarked on at Windsor with the help of William of Wykeham included the refitting of a chapel, but St George's Chapel, which is now the shrine of the Order, was not built till the time of Edward IV.

There are still twenty-five Knights of the Garter. (Members of the royal family and foreign royalties are additional to this number.) There are also two Ladies of the Garter (Queen Elizabeth the Queen Mother and

Princess Wilhelmina of the Netherlands). Queen Elizabeth II is Sovereign of the Order. The twenty-six 'poor' knights have now become thirteen 'military knights'. They are retired army officers who live with their families in Windsor Castle and attend Sunday morning service in St George's Chapel. They do not have the title 'Sir'.

The Black Death (1349) fell hardest upon those who lived in crowded conditions. The royal family did not suffer very much. Edward and Philippa lost one daughter.

Chaucer is first heard of in court circles during 1357, the year after Poitiers. Froissart arrived in 1361. They both saw the court at its gayest, enriched by the ransoms of French nobles and enlivened by the company of those, headed by King John, who had not yet found the money to pay. In the year 1364 the Kings of France, Scotland and Cyprus were all in England at the same time. Lavish entertainments were arranged.

Philippa died at Windsor in 1369 with William of Wykeham in attendance. Edward survived her for eight years. His old age was undignified, and as a result his death-bed was lonely. He was at Westminster. Towards the end his voice failed. His mistress, Alice Peers, took off his rings and left him alone with a priest. Later he regained his voice enough to whisper 'Jesu miserere' ('Jesus, pity me'). Then he kissed the cross that the priest placed in his hands and died soon afterwards. He was sixty-four. There is an effigy on his tomb in

Westminster Abbey, but to get a better idea of what he looked like at the end, you should look at the wax head in the Abbey Museum (off the cloisters). This was made from a death mask. The droop of the mouth on the left and the flattening of the left cheek were caused by the paralysis which deprived Edward of speech on the day of his death; they show that he was left-handed.

Richard II and Westminster Hall

Beside the Abbey stood the Palace of Westminster. In so far as the restless Kings of England had a permanent home at that time, this was it.

The group of buildings now commonly called the Houses of Parliament is still officially known as the Palace of Westminster; but the only part of the old palace which survives is Westminster Hall. It is worth a visit. Do not be discouraged by the notice beside the door where the queue forms for admission to the Stranger's Gallery of the House of Commons. This notice tells you that, when Parliament is in Session, the Palace of Westminster may only be visited on Saturdays. This is not the whole truth, since Westminster Hall is open every day until an hour before Parliament assembles. This means that you can go in on Monday, Tuesday, Wednesday, or Thursday from 10 a.m. till about 1.30 p.m. (on Fridays Parliament is in Session during the morning). Enter by New Palace Yard (where the M.P.s park their cars).

The first impression made by Westminster Hall is

one of stupendous emptiness. There is no single piece of furniture on all that vast expanse of flagstone pavement. Here and there a brass plate fixed in the floor commemorates some famous trial or the lying in state of Kings. At the top of the great steps (which are modern), at the south end of the hall, inscriptions commemorating the silver jubilee of George V (1935) and the trial of William Wallace (1305) are side by side.

In Wallace's time the Hall was different. The roof was lower and must have been supported by rows of pillars. Wallace was among the first of many great men to receive sentence of death in Westminster Hall. He was dragged to Smithfield on a hurdle and executed. His head, you will remember, was the first to be placed as a warning on London Bridge. This was in August 1305.

The brass plates on the floor and a framed list of names (the solitary decoration of the vast grey walls which once were brightly painted) combine to give sight-seers the impression that Westminster Hall's chief claim to fame is the fact that spectacular treason trials were held there. But such trials were rare. In Chaucer's lifetime there was none. How did Westminster Hall look to him? Certainly not empty.

Though lawyers lived and received their training further east, in the Inns of Court (p. 78), much of their work was done in Westminster Hall. The court of King's Bench occupied one corner, Chancery (the Chancellor's court) a second and Common Pleas (now discontinued) a third. These courts dealt in the main with important civil disputes, e.g. about property. The King, however, no longer sat on the 'King's Bench'. Each court had its own judges, 'men of law' (p. 159) who had reached the top of their profession.

Westminster Hall and its adjoining buildings were also the administrative centre of England. For example, the Exchequer was there. You can picture clerks laboriously calculating the revenue, using Roman numerals and an abacus (p. 65). (Arabic numerals were not introduced into this country until the sixteenth century.) Sheriffs had to come to the Exchequer twice a year bringing the taxes due to the King from their counties.

There were other departments engaged in various branches of administration. Administration then, as now, consisted of people talking things over, taking a decision, writing it down and adding up the cost. For example, Edward III, as we have seen, liked building. In addition to his work at Windsor, he had extensions made to the Palace of Westminster and rebuilt the nave of Westminster Abbey. A master mason called Henry Yevele was put in charge of the work at a salary of 1s a day. Someone had to record this appointment and see that these shillings were paid. But this was only the beginning of a vast operation of administrative pen-driving and talk. Stone had to be bought and paid for. Carters had to be engaged to transport the stone. Their wages and conditions had to be agreed. Then perhaps the weather turned bad and the carters were slow.

More argument, perhaps in words, perhaps, if the affair became serious, on parchment. Finally, were the masons ready to work on the stone when it arrived? Perhaps they had cleared off to a better job in London. A letter had to be written to the Mayor to send them back.

During his period as Controller of Customs, Chaucer must often have had business at the Palace of Westminster. His salary was £10 a year, but there was an additional grant for diligent service and other substantial sums were paid from time to time. Such rewards do not drop into a man's lap. Letters have to be written; visits have to be paid. And there were occasional expeditions abroad on government business with appropriate allowances for expenses, e.g. a grant of £26 13s 4d for a stay in France of fourteen days in 1377. Some official, knowledgeable about the cost of living in France, must have approved that payment; another official perhaps approved the approval; a clerk entered the sum in the accounts, another perhaps re-entered it in another account, a third added it up.

Parliament, which began to meet more regularly during the reign of Edward III, caused considerable clerical and administrative work. Barons, knights and burgesses had to be summoned in writing, and although their debates were not recorded, their decisions had to be written down and made known. Knights and burgesses were entitled to an allowance for expenses, but this was paid, reluctantly, by those whom they represented. It

M

177

therefore did not add to the labours of the clerks in the Palace of Westminster.

Sometimes Parliament met in towns like Gloucester (p. 167), but this was exceptional. Usually the representatives were summoned to Westminster. Sometimes the Lords and the Commons met together, in Westminster Hall, but most of their debates were conducted separately. The Commons on these occasions often met in the chapter house of Westminster Abbey, which still stands.

Westminster Hall was restless and busy, but at times it witnessed scenes of splendour. In July 1377, Richard II, aged ten, dined there after his coronation. The traditional King's champion rode into the Hall fully armed and threw down his gauntlet to challenge anyone who disputed the King's right to the throne. The challenge was repeated by a herald three times. No one took it up. Richard drank to his champion in a gold cup and presented it to him as his fee.

That was the last time that pillars interfered with the gyrations of the King's champion or with other horsemen who, for one reason or another, clattered in and out of the Hall. During his early twenties, when the Kingdom was calm for a few years and the court danced and sang in rich, fantastic clothes (p. 60), Richard ordered a new roof for the Hall.

Though Richard and his Queen were young, they chose elderly men for this work. Yevele had to undertake the heightening and buttressing of the walls. Hugh

178

Herland, a master carpenter of repute, was in charge of the roof. Had the work been commissioned a few years earlier, Chaucer might have taken part. He had been made Clerk of the Works (p. 70) at Westminster in 1389. But he only held the post for two years and it therefore fell to a successor to order timber, stone and lead, arrange transport by land and water and dispose profitably of the material salvaged from the old roof.

Work began in 1394; but in that year the young Queen died. Richard was deeply affected by her death. If she had lived, his reign might have been different.

Richard did not have much time in which to enjoy his new roof. Work was sufficiently advanced for a great feast to be held in the Hall at Christmas 1398. But nine months later the Hall was decorated for a ceremony which Richard did not attend. There was a place for him, but he could not occupy it, since he was locked up in the Tower of London. From there, he had sent a message. The Archbishop of York read it out. It was Richard's renunciation of the throne. Henry of Lancaster then occupied the empty place.

CHAPTER X

CONCLUSION

CHAUCER WAS NOT forgotten by the new King. He no longer held an official position, but Henry IV in fact paid him a larger annual grant than Richard had done. So in December 1399, while Richard shivered at Pontefract Castle in Yorkshire, Chaucer leased a house in the garden at the east end of Westminster Abbey, where Henry VII's chapel now stands (Plate XII). His wife was dead and nothing more is heard of 'little Lewis, my son' (p. 66). So the old man may have lived alone, with the monks keeping an eye on him from time to time.

On the face of it his situation was not unhappy. Town planners often remind us nowadays that old people do not like to be pushed away into a secluded corner. Many of them prefer to live in a place where there is plenty going on, where people drop in. Chaucer could scarcely have chosen a home where more varied company was available. He was within the boundary of the Westminster Abbey Sanctuary. So there were crooks as well as clerics to talk to, and debtors, and a sprinkling of genuine fugitives from injustice. Nearby, still within the Sanctuary, stood the White Rose tavern and across the way, in the Palace of Westminster, was the buzz and glamour of the administrators, the law courts and the royal household, in the midst of which Chaucer had spent so much of his active life.

So in February 1400, when news reached London that Richard had died at Pontefract, there were plenty of people with whom to gossip about the mystery. Was it murder? A disturbing thought. Nothing like it since Berkeley Castle in 1327. A very disturbing thought, if the person responsible happens to be the King who has just raised your pension. February is a bad month for disturbing thoughts; it is too dark and cold. 'When that Aprille with his shoures soote the droghte of March hath perced to the roote', life will be happier. There are pear trees outside the house. They will blossom.

In August Yevele died. Chaucer's house stood between two of the master mason's great works—the nave of Westminster Abbey and the walls of Westminster Hall. The crooks, the debtors, the monks, the tavern, and the pear trees are gone now, but Yevele's work remains. In the Abbey we can see it today as Chaucer saw it, with the stonework of the roof freshly picked out in blue and gold. He must have gone in sometimes and stared up.

But however generously nature and man may enrich an old poet's surroundings, he stares inward more than he stares up. He turns over the leaves of his conscience and wonders what death will be like. It was all very well for a man in the prime of his life to write funny stories about hell being overcrowded with friars. To the same man on his deathbed, with candles lit and the clergy moving in and out, hell seemed much less entertaining. It was at times like these that a wealthier man would set money aside to found a chantry, with a priest to say prayers for his soul. All Chaucer could do was to add a solemn prose postscript to the *Canterbury Tales,* in the course of which he wrote: 'I biseke you mekely, for the mercy of God, that ye preye for me that Crist have mercy on me and foryeve me my giltes.'

William Langland who had died not long before this (nobody knows exactly when), used a telling phrase at the end of *Piers Plowman.* 'Then he groaned after grace', he wrote. Chaucer groaned after grace, and in the autumn of 1400, only nine months after taking a fifty-three year lease of his house beside the Abbey, he died. The traditional date of his death is October 25th, two months before the end of the fourteenth century.

Chaucer had not planned his funeral with the same care as the Black Prince. It was not much use doing so, unless you were extremely rich. Whether he expressed any wishes to the monks is not known. Anyway, they buried him in the Abbey. This was not at that time an exceptional honour. It is true that certain Kings and Queens lay there, but they were in the choir, splendidly entombed. Chaucer was put in the south transept under a plain slab not far from the place where the luckless Hawle had been cut down and buried (p. 167). A hun-

dred and fifty years later a tomb was built and this can
still be seen in what later came to be called Poet's
Corner. The literary influx has not, however, been
allowed to disturb the remains of Robert Hawle. As
often happened, the brass was stolen from his slab,
but the slab is still there, not far from Chaucer, watched
by a bust of William Blake.

The Age of Chaucer

In spite of the bowmen of Crecy and Poitiers, the
stained glass of York, the alabaster carvings of the midlands, Hurland's woodwork, Yevele's architecture,
Wykeham's love of learning, Wycliffe's zeal for reform,
the beginnings of English poetry and prose, and the
introduction of tower windmills, brandy, gin and
liqueurs—in spite of all this, when writers sum up the
fourteenth century their tone is grim:

We are accustomed to regard the fourteenth century as,
on the whole, a dark epoch in the history of England—an
epoch when the corruptions and injustices and ignorance
of the Middle Ages were piling themselves ever higher and
higher; when the Black Death, having devoured half the
population of city and hamlet, was still hovering visibly
like a gaunt and terrible vulture over the affrighted country; when noblemen and gentry heard in indignant bewilder-
ment the sullen murmur of peasants awakening into con-
sciousness through pain, with now and then a shriller cry
for vengeance and a sort of blind justice; an epoch when
intellectual life was dead or dying, not only in the universities, but throughout the land/Against this dark background we seemed to see only two bright figures, that of
Chaucer, strangely kindled to radiance by momentary con-

tact with the renascence, and that of Wyclif, no less strange and solitary, striving to light the torch of reformation, which, hastily muffled by those in authority, smouldered and sparkled fitfully a hundred years before it burst into blaze. With them, but farther in the background, scarcely distinguishable, indeed, from the dark figures among which he moved, was dimly discerned a gaunt dreamer, [Langland] clothed in the dull grey russet of a poor shepherd, now watching with lustreless but seeing eye the follies and corruptions and oppressions of the great city, now driven into the wilderness by the passionate protests of his aching heart, but ever shaping into crude, formless but powerful visions images of the wrongs and oppressions which he hated and of the growing hope which, from time to time, was revealed to his eager eyes.

It is only with the 'gaunt dreamer' and his hopes that the writer of these words finds light breaking through:

That the Black Death was a horrible reality the statistics of its ravages prove only too well; that there was injustice and misery, ignorance and intellectual and spiritual darkness, is only too true; but the more intimately we learn to know the thirteenth and fourteenth centuries, the more clearly do we see . . . a host of forgotten or nameless men who battled for justice, and kindliness, and intellectual and spiritual light; and . . . *Piers the Plowman* . . . has shown . . . that that confused voice and that mighty vision were the voice and vision, not of one lonely, despised wanderer, but of many men, who, though of diverse tempers and gifts, cherished the same enthusiasm for righteousness and hate for evil.*

* J. M. Manly, in *The Cambridge History of English Literature,* Vol. II., pp. 41 and 42.

INDEX

Roman figures refer to the plates

185

Index

187

Index

Index

T

Tabard Inn, 15, 55, 97
Tables, 52-3, 56
Tables (backgammon), 146
Tapestries, 54
Teapot Hall, 44
Television, 139
Templars, Knights, 23-4, 78
Thames, River, 15, 24-5, 37
Thomas atte Chirche, 153, 165
Thomas, Lord of Berkeley, 11
Tournaments, 127
Tower of London, 179
Town planning, 39
Trafalgar Square, 21
Travel, 34-6, 169-171
Trevisa, John, 16, 68, 135
Trinity Hall, 77
Troilus and Criseyde, 142
Trumpet call (for dinner), 76
Tweed, River and Bridge, 37
Tyburn, 12
Tyler, Wat, 23, 125-7
Tyne, River, 48

W

Wakefield Bridge, 37, II
Wallace, William, 25, 175
Walbrook, 24
Walsingham, Our Lady of, 152
Wardrobes, 51
Warkworth Bridge, 37
Water-mills, 111
Weaver, the, 108, 113, 171
Weavers, 115

Wells Cathedral, 53, 86, IV
West Gate of Canterbury, 19, 127, II
Westminster, Abbey and Palace of, 14, 21, 34, 53, 86, 174-83, VIII, XII
Wheelbarrows, 115-6
Whittington, Sir Richard, 30, 78-9, 97-8, 114, IX
Wife of Bath, the, 34, 61, 74
Wiltshire, 37
Winchelsea, 39, 128
Winchester and Winchester College, 16, 34, 70-2, 86, 145, VI
Windsor Castle and Forest, 14, 36, 171-4, XII
Windmills, 111-2
Windows, 26, 43, 82
Wine, 13, 40, 56, 74, 130, 145
Woodstock, 171
Wool, 40-1, 44, 171
Woolwich, 14
Worcestershire, 43-4
Wycliffe, John, 12, 16, 70, 95-6, 140, 184, V
Wykeham, William of, 16, 34, 69-70, 84, 98, 128, 172-3

Y

Yarmouth, 130
York, 33, 37, 39, 41, 115, 140, 171, II
York Minster, 86
Yevele, Henry, 176, 178, 181